Healing the Whole

A new series of books from Cassell's Sexual Politics list,
Women on Women *provides a forum for lesbian,
bisexual and heterosexual women to explore and debate
contemporary issues and to develop strategies for the
advancement of feminist culture and politics
into the next century.*

COMMISSIONING

**Roz Hopkins
Liz Gibbs
Christina Ruse**

Healing the Whole

The Diary of an Incest Survivor

Yvette M. Pennacchia

CASSELL

Cassell
Villiers House
41/47 Strand
London WC2N 5JE

387 Park Avenue South
New York, NY 10016–8810

First published 1994

British Library Cataloguing-in-Publication Data
A catalogue record for this book is available from the British Library.

ISBN 0–304–33106–6
    0–304–33111–2

Phototypeset by Intype, London
Printed and bound in Great Britain by Mackays of Chatham plc

Contents

Acknowledgements

THIS book began as my graduate thesis at Long Island University, but before it was a thesis it was a stack of diaries and a wish. Dr Annette Zilversmit was my graduate and thesis advisor at the time. Annette, your belief in me consistently washes away the fears and clears the path to creativity. Dr Esther Hyneman, the second reader, supplied the editorial expertise. Esther, you made this project manageable through your editorial suggestions and organizational vision. Without you I might still be typing. Dr Kenneth Bernard was the third and final reader of this thesis. Dr Bernard, thank you; your insightful suggestions and quick turnaround time enabled me to hand in my thesis and graduate on time. Finally, I would like to thank two editors at Cassell: Steve Cook for accepting my manuscript, and Roz Hopkins. Roz, your calm reassurance as you answered all my questions and wonderful sense of humor made this wish come true. I cannot think of a better way of breaking the silent code of incest than to have one's work published. The secret is finally out.

*Illusions are
the family portraits of
Unwanted Realities.*

Introduction

MY recovery of my self began several years prior to the onset of therapy. In 1982, at the age of twenty-two, I realized that my father had a problem with alcohol. I never saw him drunk, but I always saw him drinking, and it took me two more years to realize the effects of alcoholism in my life. A close friend of the family recommended I attend meetings for families of alcoholics, since my father was a functioning alcoholic. For the following six months I refused to speak to this woman. In December 1984, I went to my first meeting under the guise of work. At that time I was a director of youth services in a Catholic church and many of the teenagers I worked with came from alcoholic homes. I felt it was my obligation to see how such meetings work. I was trying to save these kids when I couldn't even save myself. Three months after I began going to these meetings, I realized that I was there for myself, not for the teenagers I worked with.

During the period that I went to meetings I started slowly to defrost. I had changed jobs and was working as a hospital administrator (my current occupation), when I began to have panic attacks and great bouts of fear at work, along with uncontrollable crying spells. The attacks were what pushed me one day into the office of the Employee Assistance Program (EAP), where I asked the coordinator for a female therapist who specialized in alcoholic family systems and who was located in the city. Alicia, the EAP Coordinator, referred me to Don, who was located on Long Island. When I said that she didn't hear me, she answered, 'I know what you need, not what you want.'

Years later, Alicia told me that through her intake interview and assessment, she thought I was a rape survivor who needed a competent, loving, compassionate male therapist since a positive male role-model seemed to be lacking in my life. She knew I had dated very little and had had only one sexual encounter – with someone I didn't love at the age of twenty-four just to get 'it' over with. She sensed that I walked around encased in a thick wall.

Don's description of me at our first meeting was of an asexual young woman, covered in huge sweats, with short cropped hair, who obnoxiously grilled him in her interview. Femininity was not part of who I was and he could only speak with me by sitting at least six feet away. Not only was I asexual, but I had no feelings I could name except fear and anger, was incapable of intimacy and love, and only functioned from the neck up; I began therapy in April 1986.

During that period I attended a new meeting for families of alcoholics where I just listened. After four months, I asked Lyn to be my sponsor at the meetings, which she agreed to do even though she was shocked by my request; I had never once spoken to her. She didn't know that I had been listening to every word she said and was attracted to her strength but feared her honesty. I knew by asking her to be my sponsor I would have to *face everything and recover.* It would be another two years before Lyn would divulge that professionally she was a therapist who specialized in issues related to alcoholic families. She was starting to tell me a little bit about herself and trying to create an atmosphere that promoted intimacy.

During my first few years in the recovery program for families of alcoholics, and my first year in therapy, I focused on my alcoholic family and the effect alcoholism had on my life. Then, in July 1987 I realized I was an incest survivor. All the pain came gushing out at once and the only source of relief I had was to talk to my support group and to write what was happening. As more memories surfaced, more shame began to emerge. I became unable to talk to my therapist and the only way I could deal with my incest with a *male* therapist was to read him what I remembered and what feelings were emerging. By writing, I could put some distance between myself and my shame without stopping the process; I wrote constantly to keep up with the pain that was drowning me. My writing was the beginning of revealing the secret of childhood incest in my life. One day, Don asked if he could share my writing with one of his other clients who was an incest survivor; he thought my writing could help her. I initially laughed from shock, but then I was honored by his request; somehow my pain would help another incest survivor. This is only one example of many as to how Don has extended himself in order to help me to heal. Through the years, my relationship with Don has evolved from an emotionally powerless child to an assertive woman. As I continued to heal and share my writing with other incest survivors, I was encouraged, supported, and validated by the notion that maybe my writing could help others. I had been keeping a detailed journal for several years and had no prior thoughts of ever publishing it or becoming a writer. Although there were some books on incest that described the process, I had not come across one that revealed those many intimate steps a survivor would need to take, such as walking through the feelings of shame convinced that you are going to die, or the terror of discovering one's sexual identity that is free from abuse. It was then I decided that some day I would publish my journal and share my daily triumphs and agonies. Unfortunately, many abort the healing process somewhere between halfway and three-quarters of the way through, the point where one is required to create a new frame of reference with no blueprint to follow. Change is painful and terrifying, especially when the only thing one has known is abuse.

I believe that incest affects every molecule of one's being and the only recovery is by creating a new foundation. Today, I hope to be a source of support to other incest survivors through my writing. This road of recovery is excruciatingly painful, but the gifts are many.

Note

The names of all the individuals have been changed with the exception of Lyn and Don, who gave me permission to use their names. Marco, my uncle and perpetrator, is deceased and no longer has any power or voice in my life. Therefore I no longer have to protect his anonymity with my silence.

1987

Thursday, July 9th

● *8:50pm* ●

Tonight Don and I were talking about sex and sexuality and he said that he was 98 per cent sure that I was an incest survivor. In the fifteen months I've had him as a therapist, that's the closest to a guarantee I've ever gotten. The minute he said that, I began to hyperventilate and whimper. I told him that I've hated my father for my whole life, and I blamed him for everything, but this one was not his fault. I asked Don to tell me which was worse, being an adult child of an alcoholic or an incest victim? He said you can't compare; incest is the greatest betrayal that can happen to an individual. He wrote me this note:

'Today I have choices, (then I had none).'

As I was leaving his office, he happened to mention that we were having trouble with reimbursement for therapy. I looked at him across the room and started laughing hysterically and told him, 'Just tell them I am a fucking incest victim and you'll get all the money from here to the fucking whazoo.' Don looked sadly at me and said that was a real sick thing to say. When I told Lyn the news, she said she had known that I was an incest survivor since last October.

Saturday, July 11th

● *12:28am* ●

Dear God

Part of me knows nothing, and part of me knows something happened. While washing the dishes I felt like this tube entered my vagina and slowly glided up to my throat. My body exploded into sensations and pulsating that I've never felt before. This tube took up all the space inside. I had trouble breathing and I had to hold onto the counter so I wouldn't fall. All of a sudden, I knew I was raped by Uncle Marco while living in Italy. I cowered in the corner of the kitchen beside the garbage can in terror; I crawled on the floor to the telephone and left a message on Don's answering machine; whimpering I told him I remembered who had hurt me and could he please call me back.

Wednesday, July 15

Dear God

We had group last night, and I smoked last night and today. I realized that the sexual feelings I had with Uncle Marco were too much, too intense for a five-and-a-half-year-old to handle. I'm still having trouble breathing and I'm still tired, but a little bit more centered, maybe because I'm smoking. Don said he had to push me to the awareness of my incest because there were just so many times he could let me go down and come up for air. He said that this is it, that he guarantees that this will get better and I can't say fuck it because I've come so far. Don said he won't abandon me or betray me or abuse me. I told him I knew that, and he said I needed to hear it. He also said not to beat myself up for smoking and to be good to myself.

God

Please carry me through this and don't abandon me, help me trust you and the process.

Friday, July 17
● *7:30pm* ●

Dear God

My stomach is burning, and all I want to do is bash heads in. I told Don about the second memory I had of Uncle Marco forcing my head down to have oral sex and him rubbing his leg between me so that I'm sexually excited, that I have his penis down my throat and I'm gagging. I could only tell him about this memory by asking him to sit across the room from me, while I faced the open window and spewed my words out the window. It was too scary to tell him everything and have him sit diagonally across from me as he usually does. There seemed to be no air in the room. I cried my soul out to Don because my family didn't even notice the difference in me. Lord, I'm very angry at Uncle

Marco; he never loved me. My family wasn't able to accept me and I wasn't special to anyone. Part of me feels slimy and disgusting, and I still have a hard time breathing. Lyn said that there are still memories to come. Why can't I remember the inside of the house, or if we got caught, or when it stopped? Uncle Marco was my hero until the incest occurred. Then I shut down.

Right now, I'm depressed and sad for my little girl. She's had a real hard life. But I hope one day she'll be able to come out and play and feel safe, pretty, and special. Don said, even though parts of the incest were pleasurable and I reached orgasms it was still forced on me, because little kids don't know how to have intercourse. I also know that I love the beach today because it's open and clean, and airy, and I can breathe, and feel God's presence there. I spent a lot of time there while I was in Italy; it was the only place I felt safe while the incest occurred.

Another Time

You taught her to catch butterflies with a net barefoot in the fields. Bought her ice-cream for that cute face she made. Rafting pretended to save her from the sharks. Introduced her to the flying swings and let her ride them till she touched the stars with her toes. Kisses and hugs with dirty sticky fingers that had just finished making you mud cupcakes. Held her when she was afraid her daddy would die, dried her tears for the mommy she missed. You were her uncle but a father too. You touched her during her baths. What did she know about being fingered? It tickled. Bed tucks required licking games. Loved you with the size of a six-year-old heart. You could do no wrong. Until you raped her.

July 29th
● Uncle Marco ●

Let's make this perfectly clear. I think you're a fuckface and I hate you. You had no right to touch me. You're a schmuck. I loved you! I thought you were the best person God had ever put in my life. I felt totally safe and secure with you. I thought our hearts were attached. So much for a five-and-a-half-year-old's perception of reality. What was so special about us? We always had fun, you made me laugh, we always went to the beach together. I was totally free to be me and I felt totally accepted by you. You were my soul mate.

With the incest occurring you took a sledge-hammer and shattered everything beautiful, holy, and special about us; about you, and about me being a little girl. You killed that little girl. I'm really glad you died when you did because I don't know what would have happened next. I think God got you back for hurting me, but your death isn't enough. You died. So you got out of everything, and then on top of it you were made into St Marco. If I had my way, I'd make you come back for exactly fifteen minutes so I could personally hurt you the way you hurt me. I would start by breaking your legs and your kneecaps because it would hurt and you hated sitting still. Then, I'd make you tell my Dad so you could feel shame and humiliation. My father would finally know that you're not a saint but a sleaze bag, or better yet a scumbag, and then he would hopefully kill you; and then you would go back to where you've been for the last twenty years.

Part of me is in shock that you did it with a five-and-a-half-year-old. First of all, it was Me; and you did it in so many different positions. You used my love and trust against me. You used my body as a sexual outlet for your horniness. You never noticed that YOU were heavy, that I couldn't breathe. You never noticed my eyes, or that I was shaking from head to toe in fear and terror because every time you approached me I knew what was going to happen next. You never noticed anything about me or took into account my feelings. I was never to feel safe or secure again. You never noticed – whenever you approached me at night in my bed I would pretend not to breathe, or if I was asleep I would try to control my feelings once you woke me up. You used oral sex and fingering to get me excited so you could enter me because I had no control to fight you. I know, but I don't remember if there was force and blood involved and you just looked away. You didn't even stick around to help me clean myself. You're a sick fucking prick. I WAS JUST FIVE AND A HALF YEARS OLD! You picked on someone who is as old as my little sister Jessica.

To make matters worse, you forced me to have oral sex with you. Half of me is gagging and half of me is sexually excited, and I can't control either feeling any longer. As an adult woman I'm not able to have an orgasm; the feelings are too intense, and I'll be blown away to the moon and left there all by myself, and I won't get back. If I lose control, I'll lose it all. The sexual feelings you stimulated in me felt great, but to a certain point; after that they were too strong and harsh for a five-and-a-half-year-old. It was like having shock treatment, over and over again.

Sunday, August 9th

● *1:08am* ●

Dear God

What a great day! Antonia, Natalie, Erica, and I went in to NYC to see the movie *Nadine* and then we went to an outdoor cafe near the Lincoln Center. Lord, I named a fear today. I'm afraid of going through the process of incest because I'm afraid I might find out that I'm gay. My heart says that's not the case, but since I didn't know about the incest for twenty years what guarantee do I have that I won't find out in later years that I'm gay and just didn't know it? I need to take the risk to talk to Lyn and Don about this fear. Had this real weird dream:

Dreaming

We were on a train and every ten minutes the train would stop and everyone would run out. This happened two to three times. Stuart, this guy I like, was on the train but I ignored him. Then one time Stuart and I weren't able to run out, so we sat opposite each other at a big picnic table with many people we both knew. Stuart's legs were extended under the table and I was kneeling on them but we both looked like we were in our own seats. We knew what was going on but no one else did and it was OK and safe. Then I got up, said I had to go to the museum and ran away only to remember that I forgot my pocket book. I come back and Stuart says, 'We have to talk but you keep running away before I can talk to you.' Then this guy in a white T-shirt and crewcut starts teasing and picking on me and pushing me. I become enraged and I go for him, and start beating him up, and keep saying this won't make a dent but it's a start. The guy is running with me on his back trying to throw me off. Finally he does and runs away. In the next part of my dream, I run back to the mansion with two bedrooms that belong to two girls my age and start telling them the whole story while I'm washing my face because I have mud and dirt all over me. I'm wearing my white linen blouse and my long denim skirt. As I'm washing my face, my eyes are closed and I say 'This guy I like was there' and someone gently puts their arms around me and kisses my cheek from behind. At this point, I scream and open my eyes and it's Stuart holding me. I look in the mirror in front of me and all he has on is jeans. I then started crying and fall to the floor and so does Stuart. I said that I beat up this guy and I looked like a jerk and Stuart said, 'He probably deserved it.' And we then got up and I said, 'Can I talk to you about incest?', and that's when I woke up.

I spoke with Karen; I told her that I was angry that she had been a catalyst in the process of my realizing about the incest. I told her it was the delay in telling me; the fact that it took her three years to tell me she was gay brought up feelings of betrayal in this friendship. I need space and time. We had slept together, been camping, and I never knew she was gay. I also called Martha, the group therapist; I told her that I was angry because of the way she had handled my fear of being gay as a consequence of the situation with Karen, because she had stated that I would have to find out if I was gay or not. I spoke about my fear of finding out I was gay, as a result of dealing with this incest shit. Martha said that most incest survivors haven't dealt with their sexual development, that there's a 50/50 chance of being gay or straight, that just because I haven't dealt with my sexual development, it doesn't mean that I will necessarily come to find out I'm gay.

Wednesday, August 19th
● *10:24pm* ●

I realized with Lyn's help that I'm angry with Karen; I feel that her decision of being gay is linked to Karen not going through the process of dealing with her own experience of incest; I'm hurting and choosing to go through it. I'm also fearful of looking at my own sexuality, because shame keeps coming up. I'm afraid that I'm going to come across boobie trap number two. Maybe I'm just not ready to deal with it yet. When I feel horny, the shame comes up and I try to deny the feelings.

Wednesday, August 26th
● *10:57pm* ●

Dear God

I called Dad tonight to ask him if he could fill in some gaps about the time I was in Italy, without telling him that I'm an incest survivor. My Dad invited me out for dinner tomorrow night, and I said I'd love to go. He told me that Uncle Marco died on August 11th, and that he'd flown back on Sunday, two days later, after the burial, which I wasn't allowed to attend. Dad also told me that he was in Italy from November to June that year with me; he left me there for the summer because they didn't have enough money for my plane ticket and 'You were having a great time any way.' All these years, I had thought he had left me there by myself. Mom said the reason I went to Italy was not that I was a sickly kid, but that she had to go back to work full-time, put Annamarie in a nursery, and she couldn't support two little kids. So instead of going on welfare, my Dad took me to Italy with him. Dad and I went back to Italy because he was so sick with his manic depression that he wasn't able to work; my grandparents took care of us. God, I feel a little bit better knowing that they just didn't leave me there; my Dad said he would never have done that.

Wednesday, September 9th
• *11:00pm* •

I've just finished talking to Lyn, and between talking to Lyn and Don, I realized that I haven't been selective with whom I share the incest. I've just been dumping it as fast as I could in hope of rushing the process. Lyn said I can't be driven, but have to listen to the cues within me. Like when I decided to tell the group I was an incest survivor, I felt nauseous. That was a cue telling me I wasn't ready to talk. I'm making a conscious decision to surrender and to speak with only Don and Lyn about the incest.

Thursday, September 10th
• *10:30pm* •

Dear God

Tonight I let Don run the session his way. He wanted me to talk about my feeling about us. I came to the realization that I'm angry at him because he ripped away my denial and shattered my illusion of Uncle Marco. I also told him that I'm afraid he will go away because I'm so disgusting and have leprosy. Don said that I should only talk to him, Lyn, and Martha, the group therapist, and not talk to my friends about this. He said that I can only talk to my close friends once I've gone through the recovery process, and even then I need to be selective. He said I need my friends more today than ever and not to push them away. I don't fear that Don will physically abuse me, rather that he will be so disgusted with me that he'll just leave. I told Don that I'm angry that he knows me better than my own family does. I told him that I ignore him on those nights when we have group therapy and I see him in the waiting area – I don't want him to know me in 'real life'.

Monday, September 14th

• *7:38am* •

Dear God

As you know, I just burst out crying in the shower. In the movie *Nobody's Child*, I saw two things: if she can get through both the abuse and being institutionalized, then I can get through the incest; that there are some really good guys out there who might just be able to love me enough for me to come around. I hope I meet someone as patient as Joe, the character in the movie. I want to learn how to love.

Wednesday, September 16th

• *9:47pm* •

Dear God

I called Don tonight and he said it sounds like I'm getting through the anger phase and starting to mourn. I told Don that I'm not doing any better. He said yes I am, compared to July. I told him July didn't count because I was about to slit my wrists. He said July most definitely counted, that it's like an alcoholic who first starts sobriety; the pain counts, for that's where my recovering from incest began. When I look at it that way, I know I *am* recovering. Compared to July, I am better. I'll try to remember that pain so I won't feel sorry for myself. I guess, I'm being impatient with your time schedule God.

Saturday, September 19th

• *7:50pm* •

Dear God

Thank you for the last three days. Thursday and Friday were really excellent days at work. I was able to accomplish so much. Thursday night with Don was great too. Don said that I'm driving the bus in this process and he's just the tour guide. So I'm the one in control with dealing about the incest. We also talked about others' perception of me versus my own and how different they are. I finally admitted to myself and Don that I wasn't lovable or worth the effort; but I'm glad Don won't give up on me. Don said that the child within me gave up and thought everything was hopeless. That part of me believes Don and Lyn will give up on me any moment because I'm simply gross. But another part of me knows that's totally untrue. I'm feeling very anxious and that's because either something is coming up or because I feel vulnerable with both Lyn and Don. My adult self cares for them so very much, but my child is so afraid to be exposed because she'll get hurt, betrayed or abandoned. Lord, I'm in a funny place. I've been very horny, so my adult wants to be in a relationship and screw around, and yet my child is running the other way. I feel totally torn. Sometimes it's actually funny. Part of me is beginning to like and appreciate men and another part of me is simply terrified. This week I worked on my application for school.

Monday, September 21st
• *10:17pm* •

Dear God

I spoke to Lyn tonight about being scared, feeling horny, and the stress level that is lodged in my back and neck. She said it could be two things. It could be that something is coming up, like when I started remembering the incest in my nightmares, or it could be me 'splitting' since I'm feeling horny again and feeling like my body is betraying me.

Tuesday, September 22nd
• *11:44pm* •

Dear God

Tonight I had dinner at Julie's house and then we went to group together. At the meeting, she said she's an incest survivor, and that she doesn't know who she's going to be after this process is over. That's exactly how I feel. Something's coming up, and I don't know what. I feel like another monster is coming out and I don't know what it is all about. I spoke to Don after group and he said to trust the process and to trust him. He said we'll kill the monster and throw him off the roof and he'll be dead. My insides are racing and I'm really scared. I don't know what's going on. I told Don I wouldn't probe and I won't. I know it will come out in time, but I'm afraid I won't be strong enough to deal with it. Maybe I'll talk to little Yvette and tell her she's safe and she can tell me and I'll believe her.

Tonight, with Don's help, I came to realize that I'm afraid to let anyone in because my child self believes that if they get to know me they'll die, and if they still stick around they'll be killed by someone. A lot of pain and hurt really came up and Don held both my hands. I felt safe with him. I'm dealing with two parts of something. One is a secret and the other is shame.

Monday, October 13th
• 12:45am •
Dear God

I need to write because I'm feeling anxious. I went shopping today with Stacey and bought a dress and shoes that I absolutely love. I'm afraid because I'm finding out I don't have the power to kill someone if they get to know me, and I'm starting to wear nice clothes. I'm beginning to feel like I'm not invisible. It's a mixed bag of feelings. I'm excited and very scared. Also, I was fantasizing this week about having sex with someone I care for and love, and my adult self felt OK, but my kid self went wild with terror. Believe it or not, I feel this process is moving too fast. I'm acting 'as if' and my kid self is scared. Thank you for Stacey in my life. We're slowly getting to know each other and it's fun. Also Paradise Island is becoming a reality and if Geraldine doesn't mind I'd like to ask Stacey to come.

• 11:16pm •

Today was kind of rough. I called Lyn. I realized that I can't masturbate until I get to know my body. Lyn said five-and-a-half-year-olds normally explore their body and know themselves inside out. So I'm going to hold off on masturbating and slowly get to know my body on the outside. She also said to take showers without using a wash cloth so I can feel my skin. She said I'm working on many things, on relationships, body image, and trust; I must try to do only one thing at a time. I just started crying my eyes out because I'm feeling a lot of pain. It feels like loss.

Saturday, October 16th

● *12:25am* ●

Dear God

Just came back from a pot luck supper at Meagan's house. It was OK, but I felt kind of out of place. I saw Don on Thursday, and I told him that being an incest survivor was worse than being a dirt bag. I told him how hard it is to buy these fitted clothes. I promised him that I would buy black jeans that were a size 10 and not the 14 and 16 I usually wear. When I put them on today I felt like I had no air and told him so. He said I probably look great and I'll get used to it. I also bought a fish tank and goldfish as promised. He wants me to take care of something that is alive other than myself.

I told him about sexual urges of wanting to have intercourse. He said that's good and healthy. He said that being penetrated at five and a half years old should never have happened, and it wasn't normal, but at twenty-six that means I'm healing. He also asked me if I masturbated and I said yes. He said good and that I need to look at myself in the full-length mirror that I bought tonight. I saw myself in the mirror and couldn't believe that I was actually thin. I was pretty shocked. My first reaction was to think that the mirror was like the ones at the carnivals.

October 27th

● *12:25am* ●

Dear God

I'm tracking the process since October 16th. The following occurred: I bought a full-length mirror and I was able to see myself as thin. I felt like I'd been missing for twenty-six years. All my clothes were loose and hanging; they actually felt like they were swimming on me. I bought fitted bras and patent leather shoes, a big step towards femininity. When I spoke to Julie, I told her that my 'same here', as a response to her telling me she loved me, was not good enough and that I loved her most in the world; she's my best friend. She said whenever I tell her I love her, I'm saving her life.

Feelings of rage are being expressed through beating and stabbing pillows and crying for the last two days. I've been in intense pain, and confusion. I feel that I've lost control.

Friday, October 30th

Dear God

Last night, Julie and I met in Don's office and he role-played my healthy child speaking to Julie and then Julie's healthy child speaking to me. I was amazed how well Don knew me and how hard it was to express my feelings for Julie in front of Don. I was pretty obnoxious to Don because I felt so vulnerable and scared of being exposed. Don and I spoke about lovability, and feeling lovable, and being lovable. Don said that I have to let go of control. My feelings are safe and my denial is strong and I'm causing myself a great deal of pain. By holding onto my denial and pain, I am staying sick; and I'm not able to go further in my relationships.

Wednesday, November 4th

● *12:56am* ●

Dear God

I've been crying since Monday evening. What am I feeling? Sadness, deep pain, like someone could just step on me. I haven't been too good at stopping it at all. All I've been able to do is call people and cry. Don keeps saying, trust the process and keep reaching out. God, I'm doing it but I don't really know how much more energy I have left. Tonight on my way home from group, I came to realize that I wished Don was my older brother, and just maybe he could have stood up to Uncle Marco. Lord, I ask that you carry me through work. I also found out on November 1st that I was accepted to NYU for their certificate program in Training and Development.

November 7th

• *3:30pm* •

I got out of the shower because it was the only place where I could sob and feel safe. My Dad had called me to see how I was doing, and to tell me he was thinking of me. He said he had been really upset about Lisa Steinberg, that the father was an animal. He said he was grateful that he didn't have to worry because no one had ever hurt his kids, and if anyone had ever tried he'd have killed them. He said he cried when he heard she'd died on Wednesday. I just said, 'Yeah Dad, I know you'd kill them.' I had to get off the phone; I was sobbing and covering the mouthpiece so he wouldn't hear me, and I was leaning my forehead against the kitchen wall. I crawled back into the shower and sobbed into the tiles. What does he know? I told him about Uncle Marco when it was happening, and he didn't believe me. Dad, I could have been Lisa Steinberg.

> *Wanna Swap Stories*
>
> *Your picture. Celebrity?*
> *Dead   Blotted ink*
> *Child's soul tacked on a bulletin board*
>
> *Welts and hopelessness your trademark*
> *A seat in row S empty*
> *The lesson goes on*
> *Hugging the soil and worms*
> *removed from the blows*
> *now begin to play*
>
> *Society has awaken 25 fuckin' years too late*
>
> *Bashed skulls   bruised ribs   hung from the*
> *   window*

So you just left
had enough of the pain

I follow your shadow
knowing it could have been me.

November 9th

● *10:59pm* ●

Dear God

On the way home I cried and yelled about my parents. I kept asking them where were they. I yelled that I won't ever forgive them, and they're as responsible for the incest as Uncle Marco is. At the meeting tonight I heard that resentment and rage keep me a victim. I have to let go of the resentment by feeling my rage. I have to really feel the pain and hurt.

Tuesday, November 10th

● *7:08am* ●

Dear God

Today I have to deal with a personnel issue, and I'm shaking like a leaf. I keep thinking now they'll know I haven't been doing my job and I'll get fired. I'm really scared, and most of it has to do with the incest. I'm starting to own the fear and terror. Please help me to let it go. Lyn also said I need to feel the pain and hurt. Where is that going? It's coming out twisted. I also came to a decision not to look for a job until school is out. Part of me wants to be mad, but I can't. The decision has brought me peace. I realize that I have been sabotaging my job. Help me to be focused on my job, and keep my mind where my body is.

Saturday, November 14th

● *7:50pm* ●

Dear Dad

Dad, you really believe you know me better that I know myself? Dad you don't know shit! You lost it all when my second sister died. You've been emotionally unavailable since I was two years old. How the fuck can you know me better if I'm finding out parts of myself and my past today? You know me so well? Well did you know I was raped by your brother at five and a half years old? How about trying to picture me when I was as young as Jessica, being split open and having an orgasm. Or, getting the shit kicked out of me if I cried. Or, if I told you about the incest your brother said he would kill my whole family. Or, the fact that he use to crack my head against a wall. Or, the fact that he punched me during intercourse. Or, that I would spend hours in the bathroom cleaning myself in the bidet. If that prick hadn't died, I'd be dead. How's that for knowing me so well? Our family is fucked up. It has manic depression, chronic physical illness, alcoholism, incest, molestation, physical abuse, sexual abuse, and verbal abuse. Dad, you want to believe our life was so great. You're so self-centered. Our family had to revolve around you. Where were you the entire time in Italy when you were so sick you couldn't notice anything? On top of that, you never told me I was pretty, or intelligent. You just reaffirmed that I was bad and selfish. Well Dad, maybe I have had some real good reasons as to why my life in this family was not so great.

Thursday, November 19, 1987

• *10:00pm* •

Dear Higher Power

I saw Don tonight and he scared me. He said he would like to put me on medication because he's worried about my stress level. We rescheduled our session for Tuesday, at 7:00 pm since it's Thanksgiving week. He said he'd be able to tell by Tuesday if I needed to be put on medication. He also said that if worse comes to worse I might have to be hospitalized. Time will tell. He said hospitalization would be the last resort.

I've just spoken to Lyn and we decided that she's to come over Friday night and I'm going to let her hold me. She will be there for my adult so I can be there for my child. Higher Power, I'm beginning to feel a strand of hope. I thank you.

Friday, November 20th
• *11:40pm* •

I didn't go to work Wednesday and Thursday; I was convinced that somehow my uncle was going to rape me or kill me. I actually hardly left my room. I couldn't go out; it was too dangerous. I only went to work today because I promised Don and because he said my uncle was winning. I just called him up an hour ago hysterically crying. I told him I was cracking up, that I couldn't live one more day in this terror and if he didn't help me I was going to kill myself. I told him to get me on something because I didn't want to die. I can't live with this terror. Don called Dr Abj, the psychiatrist he works with. I was afraid I'd kill myself. I can't stop shaking and I have the sweats.

Monday, November 23rd
• *10:00pm* •

Dear Higher Power

I made the appointment with Dr Abj the psychiatrist on Saturday, and he put me on an anti-depressant and anxiety medication (only to be taken when I'm having a panic attack). Today, I was much better at work. I felt frail and in slow motion, but I was able to concentrate. I need to talk to Don about the memory of Uncle Marco punching me in the vagina over and over again, and how when Lyn was holding me I got scared and felt the anxiety of what was going to happen next. The feeling is of futility, that I won't get the benefits of recovery. That I'll die once this process is over. So I'm just stuck with the pain and I'll never know joy. Feelings of fear and then abandonment by Don and Lyn, realizing that I'm letting them in more, physically and emotionally. Shame is coming up and I'm having a hard time dealing with it with Don. Getting punched in the vagina is so humiliating.

Tuesday, November 24th
● *11:15pm* ●

Dear Don

  Tonight you acted like a real prick. As a matter of fact I called you a prick three times in group (that's a first). Who the hell do you think you are to tell me that I don't want to be nurtured and comforted. It's not a matter of choice. If I could I would. It's not that I don't want to be supported, or comforted, or nurtured; it's just too dangerous. You said that you've given me no reason to fear danger from you. Don, my Uncle gave me no reason to fear him, so I trusted him totally and I was physically and sexually abused. My perceptions of him were totally wrong and look at what it got me. Don, up to now you haven't given me any reason not to let you in, not to let you comfort or nurture me, but who's to say my perceptions aren't wrong again this time too? It's only your word, and from where I come from that means shit. And I don't really believe that you want to be there for me, especially since I'm so gross and disgusting and repulsive. What have you got to gain by being there for me? I'm writing this letter because I'm really angry, but under the anger is hurt and sadness, because you didn't believe me when I said it was too dangerous and you seemed to give up on me. Please don't give up on me. This process is hard on both of us.

Sunday, November 29th
● *1:05am* ●

  All day Wednesday I smelled a putrid odor, but now I know it was part of the incest. Also on Saturday, I woke up with my arms above my head held together and felt like my arms were being pulled out of their sockets. I know that Uncle Marco used to hold me like that so I wouldn't hit him. Help me to have the courage to deal with the pain, hurt and sadness. I want to let others in.

Monday, November 30th

• *6:30am* •

Dreaming

My Dad's sleeping with the maid in the hotel. I'm shocked. I'm wearing tough clothes. I go running to your room Don and the maid is in your room, and I scream 'You can't do that to your wife.' And you can only turn round and say 'If I have to explain to you, then you don't trust me and you don't know me.'

And I run out, and fall in front of my Dad's room just crying and helpless. You run after me and bring me back to your room and I'm sitting on the ledge against the mirror in the bathroom, and you talk to me. Finally, I tell you that I can't believe my father did that, and it goes against all his Catholic values, and I never thought he'd sleep with someone else besides Mom, and how could he do that. I believed you when you said that the maid was just in your room and you weren't going to sleep with her.

I woke up and took an anti-stress pill because I couldn't stop shaking. I felt I would be squashed if I went to work.

Wednesday, December 9th

• *7:46pm* •

Dear God

Have to write this down or part of me will deny it. I had a dream last night that I was a prostitute being pulled by my pimp who was built just like Uncle Marco. He was pulling me and I was resisting. He said I had two choices; I either put out or he would bounce me from wall to wall and I would still have to put out. I knew I had no choice and I couldn't get out. I was trapped. Also something about opening my legs on command. The word for prostitute in Italian is *putana*. I think my Uncle called me that all the time.

Saturday, December 19th

• *5:15pm* •

Dear God

Something is coming up and I still don't know what it is. But I've been crying, shaking, rageful and having the sweats. Don said he thinks the worst is out and this is just another part. He thinks my child self wants to believe it's hopeless and wants to hold onto the pain. I've decided not to see my family on Christmas Eve and see them on Christmas Day only. I can't pretend everything is fine when it's not. But I don't have to cop out and not see them at all. I have a right to enjoy the good in my life.

By talking to Julie and Antonia, I realized that I haven't processed anything that happened by telling my mother about the incest. I've been running since Wednesday, December 9th when I told to my mother. I was afraid she wouldn't believe me. She just held me and said she believed me; then I made her swear that she wouldn't tell my Dad. I shut down and ran around until Sunday. Then from last Sunday to this Sunday I've been able to feel, but the hurt, rage and guilt comes up without me realizing that some of it could be as a result of telling Mom. Backlash.

In reference to my losing weight, someone said at a meeting it was her own way of becoming that little girl again. I'm 5'10" and weigh 117 pounds. Lyn is afraid I'm becoming anorexic; I still think I'm huge.

Monday, December 21st

• *11:47pm* •

This morning I came in touch with how defenseless and helpless I was at five-and-a-half-years-old. There was no place in my apartment where I felt safe; it was just like how I felt when the incest was occurring. I was totally alone and unprotected. The only thing I could do this morning was sit in the corner of my bed and cry and shake with terror. I did remember to take the Xanex and the Tofronil. I would have given my left arm away to crawl into someone's lap who was safe, but there was no one around. Just like when I was being abused. I know that today was the first time I allowed myself to feel defenseless and helpless. Since the incest occurred, I swore I would never, ever, feel that way again. So instead of feeling helpless, I learned that if I controlled everything and everyone, I would never feel that way again. I also know now that it's so hard to be nurtured and held – it brings back feelings of helplessness, and there was no person back then who was safe for me. I had learned that I could only depend on myself, so how could I let anyone be there for me? I had let Mr Disgusting Prick be there for me, and he made me feel helpless, defenseless, hopeless, powerless.

Tonight after speaking with Lyn, I came to realize that because of the rage I felt, I was being self-destructive. I had been speeding on the highway, I had cracked the wall in the bathroom with my foot, and I was binging on sugar until yesterday.

Uncle Marco

Lyn said for me not to be like you on the bike when you killed yourself in that accident. Lyn stopped me from hurting myself. I don't want to be anything like you. I'm not about to crack the windshield, nor my own hand or foot over you. You're not worth it. So I'm going to get a plastic bat and beat the shit out of my bed, and just pretend it was you, because this rage is all inside me and it's getting out of control. So instead of acting it out or dumping it on Don or Martha, it is all going to be directed to you, the disgusting scumbag. This rage is not going to destroy me or my life. It's going to kill and mutilate your very existence. Lyn said it has to get worse before it gets better, and I'm not going to let a disgusting fuck-up like yourself do me in. You came very close, but I survived your torture and now it's your turn and I can't wait to pay you back. Just thinking about you makes my head spin from the rage I feel. I won't abandon myself or my child, because you are a disgusting prick, and I'm worth more than losing this battle.

I wish I could just set you on fire and watch you burn in agony. I can't wait until I feel indifferent about you, when I won't have to use my energy fighting the power you have over me. You're such a fuck-up, and God just wasted his time on you; it was seventeen years too long that you spent on this earth.

Sunday, December 27th

● *10:00pm* ●

Dear God

On Wednesday I saw Don and he made me realize that I'm pushing him and Martha and Dr Abj and Lyn away, but Don said he won't go away, even though I'm being horrible and letting my little kid run my life. He said my Uncle used hands to hurt, but Don will use hands to heal. That's the only way I'll come to trust again. I'm shutting the door on everyone's face. I hurt Julie by not calling her on Christmas Day, and I hurt Stacey's feelings by telling her on Tuesday night, after group, that maybe I'll talk to her and maybe I won't. Christmas night I started thinking about doom and gloom, and I got angry because I was grateful for the good time I had had during the day, and another part of me wasn't.

I finally felt the need for nurturing. I finally felt sad for my child self, and really felt the need to be held and comforted. I took a small risk and hugged Lyn tonight. Lyn is special to me. I got in touch with another myth. Lyn said she wouldn't know I cared about her through my actions since my feelings don't match my actions. I said I don't feel comfortable exposing my feelings about her to others because I fear being vulnerable and abandoned. If other people see and know how much I care about you, you will die just like my Uncle Marco did. It's OK for you to know you're special, but it's not OK for others to see my love for you.

1988

January 1st
• 2:49am •

Dear God

Thanks for a new beginning. I celebrated New Year's Eve with Erica, Antonia, and Wayne at the Clean & Sober party, wearing the black dress with the V back and the big bow and train. I looked really beautiful. I jumped up and down when the New Year arrived, because even though last year was filled with a lot of intimacy and love, it was filled with a lot of pain too. I have a great weekend planned: sleep late, have dinner at my parents' house, get my hair cut, go to the Museum of Natural History with Karen, and then go to the movies to see *Empire of the Sun*, have brunch with Stacey and Kevin, and go to Jessica's birthday party.

Tuesday, January 5th
• 9:59pm •

Dear God

My Higher Power is speaking to me through my gut, and I have to trust that school, work, and moving will work out just the way they're meant to work out. I need to trust in the goodness of my Higher Power and the goodness of my life today. I also understand what Don means when he says I abandon my child. When I feel hopeless, the adult leaves the child and I revert to being five-and-a-half-years-old again and not believing in the good, or that things will change for the better. I must leave my child in the past. When Don simply complimented me on how I looked, my skin was clearing up and I looked very feminine, I got scared and plugged my ears and told him to stop. I feel like he's lying, even though I know he's not. I then went out at 2 in the morning to a '7/11' to buy cigarettes, and a Ring Ding which I ate; I sabotage myself by eating sugar.

I do want to believe Don, but I'm scared.

Sunday, January 10th

I spoke with Julie today about the hard time I'm having talking to Don about low self-esteem, shame, sexuality, and issues about being a woman. Julie said that I have to remind myself of Don the therapist and not Don the man. Part of the struggle is because he complimented me on Thursday and I thought of him as Don the guy. I know he's just trying to teach me about myself and about guys, but I feel like I'm out of control and there are no boundaries. I guess fear is coming up. I realize that Don is really not the issue but owning my issues myself is the problem; my own issues of sexuality, sexual drive, and attractiveness bring up the feeling of being out of control. And maybe I can begin to talk to Don about the feelings of being out of control. I'm in a lot of pain. I told Don I'm afraid to face myself. I don't know something that my unconscious knows. It might just be sexual conflict, or I might be gay and not know it yet. All I do know is that I've been crying and pain is coming up rather quickly. I hate this process and I feel I'm going to come across some more monsters. Give me the strength and courage to deal with this, whatever the pain is and help me face myself.

Saturday, January 16th

• 12:27am •

Dear Don

Part of me feels very sad. I truly don't believe that any guy could find me attractive. If by some miracle he did, I'm almost positive he wouldn't stick around for as long as I would need him to in order to trust and feel safe with him before I had sex with him. It might take years. Don, I trust you but I don't feel safe talking to you about sex; part of me believes that I'll say something that will make you snap and you'll attack me physically and sexually. In my head I know that's not true, but I do feel this way.

I also feel like I'm entering the danger zone. I'm having trouble breathing and I'm feeling out of control. I really believe that somewhere, somehow, sometime, all this abuse will be repeated. Most guys are bigger and stronger than I am, and could hurt me sexually. So I'm probably destined to live alone my whole life. I'm caught in the middle with no way to turn.

As much as I don't want to live alone is as great as my fear of doing so; both only bring pain. I feel isolated and my sexuality only brings on pain, so therefore it's been better to negate my sexuality. I think that if I were to stop therapy today and go back into denial I could continue intimate relationships with both men and women. But I would live alone, have no sexual involvements whatsoever, and just masturbate when I couldn't deny my sexual feelings. I know that much about myself for today. Physical contact (longer than ten seconds) produces fear, and I'll think to myself 'What's going to happen next?' If I let you hold me and I drop my guard, then something bad will happen. Don, two weeks ago you said that there's no need to tell the guy I might marry that I'm an incest survivor because it won't be an issue. Don't you think he might notice how I just shut down or start shaking from head to toe, and think there might be something fucked up. Part of me just wants to scream at you because I think you're leading me on. Don't tell me anything unless you know it is possible and attainable, because I'm going to start not believing anything you say.

When I was five-and-a-half, I wasn't treated as a child. Today, if a guy were to get involved with me sexually he would be dealing with a scared five-and-a-half-year-old. I don't know if it's possible to go back and rebuild on a shattered foundation. A shattered foundation won't hold up a structure; my foundation was blown away by the incest and the violent physical abuse. So there's really nothing there but a mind, emotions, a soul, and feeling horny. Nothing to build on for a normal intimate sexual relationship with a man. If I could, I would shoot my uncle. One finger and toe at a time. His knees, his shins, balls, arms, stomach and face. I would do it slowly, so he would be conscious and only die once I was able to blow his head off.

With reference to my fear of going through this process, finding out I'm gay is more than I could handle. My father sees homosexuality as a moral issue. If I were to find out I was gay, I couldn't act on it; I would rather be celibate my whole life. My thought of being sexual with another woman is, first, that it would be pretty boring and, second, definitely repulsive. I have no understanding of living that way. It's not a moral issue for me; it's more an issue of acceptance, the issue of accepting myself, and also accepting society's stigma. Already, I feel like a reject and outcast. If I found out I was gay, life wouldn't really be worth living. I wouldn't kill myself; I don't think I ever could accept it.

I read this letter to Lyn and she said I'm afraid to be nurtured because my guard will come down and I'll crumble. I feel a little bit safer with Lyn, but not safe enough to be nurtured because she's the adult, and when I am nurtured I feel like the child. Lyn said I've backed off from her emotionally since I let her hold me. It was just too scary, but I hadn't realized I was slowly backing away. I haven't allowed an adult to nurture me since the incest occurred.

The only reason why I allow Julie to nurture me is because she's my five-and-a-half-year-old pal. She's not an adult, she's my best friend. I don't trust adults not to hurt me.

Lyn says it doesn't count when I kiss and hug her because I'm the one who's in control, but even so, I shake every time. She said I have to lose control in order to be nurtured. If I won't let Lyn in who is less threatening, I'll never let you in Don. Don, if I don't let you in, I won't ever be able to have a normal intimate relationship with a guy. If I can't trust you and Lyn who else can I trust? I'm really scared about all this and I'm stuck. I'm stuck, physically and sexually, at five and a half years old when the incest occurred, and I have no idea how to move forward.

Monday, January 25th

Dear God

I had to write this dream down, because it scared me so much. Last night, I was really thinking and believing that a healthy, intimate relationship is possible for me in time and yet I still had this dream . . .

Dreaming

I was married to a normal guy and we were happy. The next scene in my dream is that I'm in my late thirties, and I have an eleven-year-old girl, a nine-year-old boy, and a seven-year-old girl. Overnight, my husband becomes an alcoholic. When I realize that, I tell the kids to run to the car and leave. As they do my husband sets the nine-year-old boy on fire. I put the fire out, put the kid in the car, and take off. I'm running away.

That's when I woke up and I couldn't stop shaking. I tried nurturing my kid, but it took a while before I could calm down.

Thursday, January 28th

• *6:30pm* •

Lyn has asked me to write about the need of intimacy with Lyn and Don. Last Thursday's session with Don, telling him what qualities I was attracted to, somehow was like turning a key and letting the need of intimacy out. Like Lyn says, 'You have to want to want it.' Lyn says that I'm still backing away from intimacy with her by being scattered in my sharing and hopping around. For some reason I get to a certain point of intimacy with Lyn and Don, and then I hit a barricade and run the other way. Lyn wants me to write about intimacy with herself and Don and what it means to me. When I think of Lyn and Don, I think of a deep level of intimacy and yet I know that there's a deeper level that can be obtained. Up to this level it's been hard and scary. But it's nothing compared to the fear I feel, which is being physically and emotionally available on a deeper level with both.

I look at this level of intimacy as terrifying. It brings up feelings of ownership and loss of power on my part. If I make myself this vulnerable to them, they will own me and can do what ever they want to me. I lose all my power over who I am. Also the control and power will be in their hands and I will be owned both body and soul. That's why with some people I'm either emotionally available or physically available; to put both with one person makes me feel like they will have total power over me and

I will not be able to protect myself. As a five-and-a-half-year-old I was emotionally open to my Uncle and physically affectionate to him; by being that intimate, he crossed all those boundaries. He had all the power and control and I was owned. I became his slave and he had the power to decide if I lived or died. If he hadn't died, I would have died.

Sunday, February 7

● *11:35pm* ●

Tonight I saw Don, and I finally felt the pain, hurt, and some anger and rejection I've been feeling toward Julie by her shutting me out. It really hurt a lot and I withdrew from Don. I was in too much pain, and I didn't want Don's comfort because I didn't want to cry; if he held me I'd cry even harder. My little kid doesn't feel too lovable and Don said I can't let someone else decide if my child is lovable or not. He also said that I've been hit in the stomach by Julie and that's why I'm having a hard time trusting Lyn and Don. He said it might be time to branch out to new relationships. I'm really pissed off that he said that.

Sunday, February 14th

● *4:45pm* ●

Dear Higher Power

I spoke to Don about my fears of owning my sexuality and talking to him about it. I'm still afraid that somehow he'll attack me as a result of me talking about sexuality. Don said that he's attracted to some of his clients; I said it's because he knows them. He said no, he meant sexually; I said he couldn't be. He said he is, but he doesn't act on it. His ethics, trust in the process, and dealing with his clients, are stronger than his impulses and his desires; but he doesn't leave his sexuality at the door when he comes in. It's part of who he is. He then told me he was sexually attracted to me. I told him he was stupid. He couldn't stop laughing when I called him stupid.

Part of me is scared because he said he was attracted to me, and another part of me was shocked that he could find anything sexually exciting about me in general. Even more so because he knows my history. Part of me is tickled pink that he's attracted to me; maybe I can't be that rotten. And yet, Don, my feelings were really hurt on Saturday. When I told you that I was still afraid to talk to you about sexuality. You said, 'What did you think would happen? I'd turn into a hairy ape and chase you around the room?' Then you started to laugh, you made fun of me. My fear is blocking the process.

Don, if I don't get over this fear with you, you can forget about me ever dating. I trust you the most of any man I know, and I'm still afraid of being attacked or raped by you. Don, I couldn't feel the pain and fear from the abuse because my grandparents would notice. So I slept in the bathroom in the tub whenever I could. I don't know Don, but the experiences of my childhood with my uncle more than justifies my fear of you. Don, my first introduction to sex and sexuality was incest. You can laugh at the fact that I'm dealing with sexuality twenty-one years later, and I still feel the fear that you might attack me.

You've given me no reason to fear you, but neither did my uncle until it was too late. I think you're wanting me to move a lot faster than I really can. If I'm still afraid or can't look in your eyes while talking about sexuality, what in your right mind makes you think I could handle a date? I also wish you hadn't said anything about being attracted to me. I don't believe it is at all possible and it also feeds right into the fear. I don't want you to say anything like that for a while, nor compliment me on what I look like or am wearing, because I don't see or hear it for what you mean. I just hear it as a ploy. The words are hollow and I feel you have an ulterior motive. I know none of this is true, but I'm not there yet where I can separate you from the past. I'm scared and I'm stuck and I'm afraid that this process will end without me ever fully trusting you, or being able to give you a hug like I hug Julie or Lyn. I'm really scared because I think the incest is going to win over the process.

I read the letter to Lyn and she said that I might be minimizing my fear and lack of trust of you when I'm in session. I am, because I don't want to say or trigger something in you that might make you flip out and attack me. I feel ashamed. I know that I'm more afraid of physical abuse than sexual abuse from you, but I'm still afraid of both. Don, you also said that it wouldn't be therapeutically sound if I hopped into bed with some guy. Don, I don't think you're really hearing how scared and stuck I am in dealing with guys. When I told Lyn, Martha, and the group, that you said I should go on a date with the guy from work, Lyn and Martha totally agreed with me that it wouldn't be a good idea. Don, you're talking giant steps, and I haven't even learned how to sit up, never mind crawl.

Also I think your time frame in this recovery process is totally off. Can you really sit there and tell me that my incest issues won't be an issue by the time I get married and I will be able to view sex as fun and healthy and adult play? Don, you might be right if I'm planning to be married in my forties and never have any kids. I'm not too sure you are reality based at all where I'm coming from. Maybe I'm putting up a good front, because I don't trust you. Don, I'm trying to be as honest as possible with you, but I'm getting the feeling that you think I'm at a better place than I am. The bottom line is that I don't trust you totally yet, and that's what is stopping this process. I don't believe that now that you know my personality, my gross insides, which somehow have crossed over to my gross outside, that I'm safe with you. I don't feel safe with you at all.

But you know what's the weirdest thing of all? Even though I don't feel safe or trust you totally, I'm kind of missing you while you're on vacation. I really don't understand this at all.

February 25th
● 9:45pm ●

Dear Higher Power

Tonight when I spoke with Don, he said he thinks I was secretly in love with Christopher. Don said adults from alcoholic families have a hard time integrating sex, sexuality, intimacy, and attraction. As I was riding home, I started thinking about Christopher. I think I *was* in love with Christopher; actually I know that today. I decided to write down some memories:

• I met Christopher in 1977. He was on a bike, said 'Hi', and rode away.

• First time I got drunk, he literally carried me home because we were in high school and couldn't drive.

• He drove me home in his Volkswagen and bucked the whole way home, but ran out of gas in the rain, and I made him go to gas station by himself.

• He ruined his Volkswagen because he didn't know he had to put oil in it, and I ruined my Bug's engine six months later for the same reason.

• In college we spent so much time together and got along great. We used to say the only thing we didn't do was sleep together.

• He fell in love for the first time and she just used him.

• He leased his friend's apartment for the summer and he told me that he learned in his sexuality course that he was in the 0.2% for males over twenty who were still virgins. We laughed and he swore he'd never get married.

• He took me out for my twenty-first birthday to Swenson's and I let him buy everything at the Miracle Mile because we were window shopping. I even picked out lingerie I wanted and he couldn't believe I really liked that stuff because I dressed like a college guy who is into athletics.

• We worked retreats together and we were dancing to Rock Lobster and he wrenched his neck and wore a scarf around it the whole weekend, and I would burst out laughing every time I looked at him.

• I went to visit him on our twenty-fifth birthdays and it was the first time I felt funny being in a bathing suit around him. He took me to every *Ann Taylor* in town so I could buy their winter clothes on sale, but I made him wait in the mall, and wouldn't model any clothes. I told him to get lost when I got to the store, and he didn't get angry or rush me.

• I finally convinced him to stop being a chicken shit and ask his future wife out, and a month later he asked me if he was overdoing it by seeing her thirty out of the thirty-one days. When I asked him how he felt about it, he said great and I told him fuck it then and have a great time and we laughed.

Tonight, driving home, I realized for the first time that Christopher has great looking legs, and it only took me ten years to realize that. When I had just started therapy with you, Don, I called him in San Francisco and cried for forty-five minutes after I told him about the incest, and told him I really hated that he lived so far away, but that I was glad that he was there for me. When I spoke to him last month and he told me that he loves me, I started to cry and I told him that I knew that but he had never said it before. He used to call me his shadow because we ran in the same circles; when I finally blew up and told him that I hated that nickname, he said if he had really minded he wouldn't have spent so much time with me and that he wouldn't call me that anymore. When I told him about Richard and not being a virgin any more, he was shocked, but happy and surprised that I told him. He acted like a prude and an old fart.

Don, you're right. I was in love with Christopher and didn't even know it until you said it. The minute you said it, I knew it was true.

Sunday, February 28th

● *10:30pm* ●

Dear HP

I'm feeling sad. There's a sadness and loss over Christopher. Maybe I'm going through mourning or regretting that I wasn't capable of letting Christopher in physically, and that neither was he. Part of me feels lucky that Christopher was a part of my life, but part of me is missing him more right now than ever before. Part of me wishes I was ready to love a guy physically and emotionally right now. Maybe this realization about Christopher is to give me hope. I wish I could crawl on Christopher's lap and just let him hold me right now, but that's not really possible any more. Christopher, you were my first love and I only found that out these past couple of days. I feel like my guts have been shot out.

Today I fantasized about having sex with Christopher. I know that I never had any sexual feelings towards him because I was sexually repressed and so was he. And I know that if today Christopher wasn't married and still lived here, I would see if our long intimate friendship could change so that we could be lovers as well as intimate friends. Don, you said I was really lucky to have Christopher in my life, as a friend, to learn that guys are good and nice and safe.

I let myself own the feeling of being in love with Christopher, not deny it and let myself fantasize about having sex with Christopher. It was so real. I got a glimpse of sex being fun. In my fantasy I was really assertive and didn't lie there like a piece of cardboard. I know exactly what he looks and feels like with no clothes on. I even bit Christopher's thigh and wasn't afraid of his penis because I know, love, and trust Christopher, and he feels the same way about me. In my fantasy, I allowed Christopher to enter me and kept reminding myself that this was Christopher and not my uncle, and yet even in my fantasy I was getting really scared and shutting down.

So I said to myself, what would Christopher say if this was really happening? I heard Christopher say while he was in me to relax, and it's not going to be fun or sexually exciting for either one of us at this point, and that getting rid of the fear was the first hurdle. He then very slowly withdrew his penis most of the way and very slowly entered me. He did this about six times and while looking into my eyes he kept reminding me that he was Christopher, the person who was my friend and loved me and wouldn't hurt me. I should just try to feel him entering me and withdrawing. It felt really soothing and stimulating, but I was still getting scared. So I rolled over and got on top of Christopher and I controlled the movements, but I still continued to get scared. So Christopher told me just to rest and lie on top of him, while he was still inside me and he would hold me until I wasn't scared anymore.

● *11:40pm* ●

I read Lyn my letter about fantasizing about Christopher. I was really scared and felt ashamed but relieved after I read it. Lyn said the shame might be coming from the fact that I might have enjoyed parts of the incest; how could I want to have sex like that, especially since my uncle called me a *putana* during it. Maybe I feel that I am one by owning my feelings on some level. Maybe I feel that's true.

Thursday March 3rd

● *11:43pm* ●

Dear Higher Power

Don said he looked like Christopher when he was in high school. Don also said that he thinks I'm sexually attracted to him, but that I'm not being honest with myself. Lyn said that if I do admit to being sexually attracted to Don, what am I afraid of? Everything will change. I'll become even more self-conscious and my walls will go up and everything will change. I think Don is probably right, but I'm not willing to admit this to myself. Today I didn't go to work. I was just angry and depressed. Don said good; it's getting better.

Friday, March 4th

● *11:45pm* ●

Dear HP

I was masturbating and fantasizing having sex with Christopher, and I kept going to the point of climax and would hit that wall and couldn't go over the edge. I was afraid to let go of control with Christopher, the one guy I loved and felt most safe with. I couldn't even reach the point of orgasm in my head because of fear. My uncle contaminated even that part of me where the soul touches the sky, or if you're really lucky where you and the person you love touch the sky at the same time. I couldn't stop crying because he even destroyed that part of me that isn't physical; he contaminated my soul.

Monday, March 7th
● *9:59pm* ●

Dear HP

Today was a great day at work, but tonight I was really depressed and mourning over Christopher. I feel like Christopher died. The thought of Don hearing my fantasy about Christopher really kind of makes me want to die. I know I have to, but I don't want to and the thought of hugging Don afterwards really makes me ill and squirm. I just finished speaking with Lyn and I don't know if I can read the letter to Don, but he'll have to read it. Lyn said that maybe I think this is a sin.

I realized today that somewhere deep down I believe if you're spiritual, you don't feel these strong sexual feelings. So if I'm feeling these feelings I must be bad and maybe my uncle was right. I am a whore. Intellectually I know just the opposite is true, but that's where it ends. Besides feeling totally exposed, after Don reads this letter I'm afraid that he really will know how bad I am and just maybe I'm at fault for what happened.

Saturday, March 12th

Don read my letter about fantasizing having sex with Christopher, and I did hug him. The shame came up so strongly that I didn't even lift my neck in session. Don said my fantasy isn't like 'Debbie does Dallas' but rather more like *Love Story*. He said my fantasy was an example of love and caring that many couples could learn from in the bedroom. Don said something really nice: he was really glad that I had let him in emotionally, and it was time to take a break from this process and to lighten up. I still have to go to meetings, therapy, group therapy, and call Lyn, but the next session with Don, we're going to have pizza and come back to the office and talk about interesting stuff.

Don said sharing my fantasy about having sex with Christopher was a major breakthrough because it dealt with sexuality, sex, intimacy, and trusting Don too. I know the only reason I let Don in was so that some day I could let a guy in emotionally and physically and let him be part of my life. It wouldn't be a missed opportunity like it was with Christopher and me. Even though I was scared, if I didn't make myself vulnerable, my uncle the disgusting prick would win. I would rather die a little bit by letting Don in, than have Mr Prick himself win. Don said my uncle is losing the battle really fast, and one day I'll be able to kick over his tomb stone and even piss and shit on it. I started laughing because if I did do that, my uncle would only get what was long overdue. I can't wait until the day when he has no power over me and I can finally kill off his ghost. God, how I hate that man.

Sunday, March 20th
● *11:31pm* ●

Dear HP

Today is the first day of Spring. This morning I was at Julie's at 9:30. We bought tickets to go to the circus. We were nine rows from the floor right in the center. We laughed and screamed and acted like five- and six-year-olds instead of two twenty-seven-year-old women. It was great. I'm really glad I took this weekend off to just play and not deal with anything that is painful, or my recovery.

Sunday, April 3
● *10:35pm* ●

Dear HP

I've been running away again. I haven't taken the time to write down the feelings because I don't want to face them. I spoke with Don Thursday night, that I'm shaking again because eating together is too close to dating. I'm really scared because the process is working and I am letting Don in. I told him I'm afraid to let my wall down with him because I'm afraid I might come to care for him too much or fall in love with him. Don said if I should feel that way we'll deal with the feelings and by letting Don in I'll be able to love a guy someday. Don said my wall is almost gone and it's just made of tissue paper. I also wore my favorite shirt to his office because I came to believe that Don wouldn't attack me if I looked attractive.

Last night, I realized that I really let Don in more than I care to admit to myself, and that I'm probably in love with him but not ready to admit it to him or myself. Right now I'm in an awful lot of pain. I saw Lyn at the meeting and my eyes got tearful because I feel vulnerable with her.

Monday, April 4th

● *12:02am* ●

Dear Don

I'm writing this down so I won't go into denial and Lyn said that I should speak to you about it. Lyn believes, and so do I, that I'm stuck and I can't become any more intimate with her at this time. She says there are just so many times she can go on pointing out that I'm running away from her.

She feels that the time may just not be right for me to go any further with her; I'm unconsciously putting people, places, and things in the way by calling when I know she can't talk or by being too busy to call her at all. She doesn't feel it's fair of her to push me into becoming intimate with her if I'm not capable at this time. She says that I might be afraid of abandonment by her, or that maybe she's not meant to be the person I let in. She says all my energy is going towards working with you and letting you in and feeling safe with you.

I said, so by letting you in I lose Lyn? She said it's not a loss but a growth because you're a guy and I'm letting you in. I know I've put her and Julie on hold. I think I'm willing to let Julie back in while I let you in, but I know I'm not letting Lyn in right now. It's just too crowded in my soul and it's bringing such great fear that I'm not eating or sleeping. I started to cry really hard – Lyn's letting me go so that I can decide if I want to be intimate with her by my choosing from within and not her pushing. She says that the timing may be off or it's not meant to be.

Don, I feel really sad, and I can't stop crying, but I know I can't let you in and Lyn in as well. It brings up too much terror. I know if it's meant to be, she'll be waiting for me, but I don't feel that. I'm so afraid. Don, I've let Lyn in so much and now I can't go any further. I told Lyn, if I don't let her in I'll never be able to be intimate with someone, and she said that's not true. It can mean the time is off or that she's not meant to be the one. Don, this pain really hurts, but I can't push any harder. I guess I do have to let go of Lyn until I feel safe with you.

Somehow I feel like I've lost something really big like a piece of my heart and yet I'm not able to let her in no matter how I try. She said she's not abandoning me. I have to want intimacy, and she feels I don't just now because I'm running from her. She said that my relationship with you and Julie might be all that I can handle right now.

Don, what do I do? I'm so confused and lost and I can't stop crying. She said that I can call her based on my needs. I know that she's not abandoning me, but that is what I feel. She said I'm trying so hard not because I really want it but because I'm supposed to be doing this. Don, I wish you were here right now so I could figure out what to do. I'm really scared of losing Lyn, but I still won't let her in.

● *11:05pm* ●

I spoke to Don about Lyn and he said I'm acting out two rules that my uncle, the disgusting prick, taught me on a verbal and non-verbal level. The first was that as a kid I felt he owned me so I could only have one intimate relationship at a time. He was the only one who was that intimate with me. Secondly, I can't let my guard down with physical affection because the physical part of the incest was a secret too; my uncle said if I told anyone he would kill my family. So with physical intimacy I can only express it to one person (being owned) and not in public (keeping the secret).

I told Don that Lyn has come through every door, but this last door is metal and I don't have the keys to let her in. I'm afraid to let her in while I'm working on letting him in. Don said I do have the keys but when I start running I turn the keys over to my uncle and he is then running the show. I also realized that when I let only one person in then I give them all the power, just like my uncle had over me when I was five-and-a-half-years-old. If I let Julie, Don, and Lyn in then there's sharing and they don't have any power. I have all the power. I'm breaking all the rules my uncle made up for me. This stupid process is working again. Don told me to ask Lyn if her feelings were hurt by my running away.

I realized while I was crying my eyes out in Don's office that I want Lyn as part of my life and need her too. I was projecting what-ifs to Don and he told me to stop. I only have two choices: to let Lyn go, or to stop running and let her in. I told Don both choices stank. He told me that I needn't try to control things all the time; the process is hard enough, but that I make it harder. I told Don that I told Julie last week that I needed her and she's the safest of the three. It would be even harder to tell Lyn. I got home and prayed for courage to call Lyn. She was free. I told her that I cried more over her than anyone before who was a part of my life. I told her what Don said about my uncle the disgusting prick, and I asked her if her feelings were hurt.

Sunday, April 24th
● 11:36pm ●

Dear HP

I called Christopher tonight, and I spoke with him about my awareness of realizing I was in love with him for all the years I knew him, that I was ignoring him because of the awareness and pain. Christopher said that he knew that I was ignoring him, that he'd decided to keep calling me on a monthly basis, that he knew I'd call him eventually and let him know what was going on. Christopher said he'd realized that I was in love with him two and a half years ago while in therapy himself, but I had to come to that realization myself. I asked him if he was in love with me; he said to some extent yes and that our relationship was safe, and he was glad I had come to that awareness as well for myself. I told him I had to tell him because it was a positive experience for me, and he was a special man in my life. My only fear was that it could endanger our present friendship, but that if anything it might make our friendship stronger, and he said definitely. I also told him I love him a lot, and he's my pal, and he's really special to me.

After I got off the phone, I called Lyn because I was relieved but a little scared by the big risk I'd just taken; I needed to talk to Lyn because I was feeling exposed and a little bit unsafe. I didn't lose Christopher as a friend. Maybe I had to go through the awareness of being in love with Christopher and letting go of our past so I could now begin to move forward maybe with some other guy.

Wednesday, May 4th

Dear Don

At 4:30 this morning I woke up and couldn't go back to sleep because of an awareness I had. I got a picture of my insides behind that metal wall and it was dark and quiet like a museum. In it was Julie running around like little kids do, and Lyn was being the quiet and gentle adult she is and simply walking around. But all of a sudden it was like a formal ceremony, and I consciously let you in. There was a great deal of acceptance and peace. I felt I won a major battle.

Last night someone in group said that she didn't want to be in group because she would have to face her womanhood. That's such a stupid word, and I hate it. I like Leo Buscaglia, because he says 'personhood'. I've been facing my personhood since high school, on one level or another, but I've avoided facing my womanhood at all cost and that has probably been my greatest battle with you. Just because I've let you in, that doesn't mean I'm ready to talk about my womanhood.

Saturday, May 7th

• *1:16am* •

Dear HP

Don said a miracle occurred in his office by me admitting that I loved him and letting him in behind the wall. He said he felt very privileged – he was the first man I'd let in because, he said, Christopher was part of my past and not physically here. Right now I'm crying and it's hard to write; some of the tears are of sadness but some are of disbelief that Don should feel privileged. I find it hard to believe he really feels that way. I know he does because he wouldn't lie to me, but part of me is simply in disbelief that he could know so much about me and still care and not run away or hurt me.

After I read Don my letter telling him about loving him and letting him in he asked me how I felt. I had brought my teddy bear to therapy, and after I shared with him I just held on to my bear and became a five-and-a-half-year-old again and I started to shake from head to toe. I told him that I was afraid now that he knew he'd turn into a monster. Don told me he wasn't my uncle and he wouldn't move one inch out of his chair except to give me his bear so that my bear would have company and remind my child that he was safe.

When I told Don about blame and shame coming up as a result of my need for affection he said that was because my child believed that the abuse was affection. Don told me that my uncle was sick, that the need to be held and comforted was good. He was also really glad that I was going to Paradise Island. He said it was a good sign and that I was getting on with my life. Some of the horrible feelings were beginning to fade. He said one of the biggest miracles he saw in me was that I was able to buy fitted clothes in the middle of all the pain of the process. I told him my binoculars weren't working so well and it was getting harder and harder to be invisible. I asked him what to do when I want to be invisible and some guy is staring at me and I start to feel scared. He said to move closer to someone I feel safe with. Lyn said I could always call someone.

Wednesday, May 18th

• *11:26pm* •

I can't believe I haven't written anything in ten days, but in a way I can. So much has happened. I'm three-quarters packed for moving into my new apartment and that's been taking a lot of time, plus I've been working overtime a lot. Tonight I worked until 9 pm, and it took me an hour and a half to get home because the roads were flooded.

Even though I've been home just three days from Paradise Island, I feel like the trip was months ago because work is crazy. I felt safe enough to let my little girl out; she was having so much fun that she started to shake because she believed that something bad was going to happen, but I comforted her and told her she was entitled to have as much fun as possible because she deserved it and no one was going to hurt her. It was exactly what I needed, we giggled and laughed and just relaxed.

Wednesday the day before we left I almost called Don three times but I didn't because I knew it was just the old myth. I felt that now Don knew I loved him, somehow he was going to die while I was away, but I was able to comfort my little girl; I told her that just because my uncle died it didn't mean that if she shared her love with Don, he would die too.

Friday, June 10th

• *11:39pm* •

Dear HP

Thank you. Right now I'm a little teary-eyed because I'm feeling joy. I love my new apartment. It's so cozy, safe, and cute. There's so much to catch up on. Last night when I saw Don, the session was hard. Don said that in fact I had remembered the first time the incest occurred and also what led up to it. Don read me back a letter I wrote in July of last year. It said that my uncle fingered me and had oral sex with me. Don said it is biologically impossible for a six-year-old's vagina to be able to hold a penis without any preparation. He said my uncle seduced me because the relationship I had with him prior to the incest was like one of a soulmate and that is not appropriate behavior between an uncle and a niece. He said the incest probably started with tight hugs and rubbing my stomach and then fingering me and oral sex. Don said this probably happened several times before the rape actually occurred.

I told Don that I don't remember the first time it happened. He told me that I had become unblocked in his office and I became that five-and-a-half-year-old child with blood on the sheets, who was all bruised and battered, and I had to go to the bathroom and clean myself off. I told Don that he must have me confused with someone else's story, because I don't remember any blood nor do I remember telling him about it. I kept insisting he was mistaken.

When the session started and Don told me about the blood and bruising, I didn't believe him and my trust level in him dipped to near zero, and during the session I tried to get angry at him and debate with him, and he said he wouldn't fall in my trap, because I was trying to get angry at him, push him away and cause pain in our relationship; so instead he made me laugh at myself by showing me how awful I've sometimes treated him. Don said I can't remember the blood because I was reliving the experience as a five-and-a-half-year-old in his office. He said that there were times when I cried and was in so much pain and shock that if I was older, I could have gone into cardiac arrest. When I asked him to tell me what I couldn't remember he said no, that there was no reason to bring all that pain and agony up again.

I asked Don why I took a nose-dive from Sunday to Wednesday. I couldn't breathe. Why did I have the sensation of that tube in my vagina to my throat? The only time I felt that was the first time I became unblocked last July. Don said there were several times I shared that sensation with him in therapy because I felt that was how much space my uncle's penis took up within me. I told Don I don't remember sharing that with him, except the first time last July. Don said what I experienced this past weekend was a flashback, not one of memory, but of being overexposed. He said I felt overexposed because I'm working on relationships and getting to be friends with Stacey and spending the day at the beach with her. He asked me how I felt in a bathing suit. I said fine. He asked me if any guys had checked me out. I said I didn't know; I wasn't looking or counting. He said on some level I knew guys were looking at me. He said I probably looked great in a bathing suit, and guys thought so too. When he said all this I told him to stop because I couldn't breathe. That's when I knew that it was a flashback and not something like a big monster becoming unblocked.

Don said if anything is to come up it will be nowhere near like last summer, fall, or winter. Don said that I've let my panic and fear run my life during the past few days, that my panic and fear are my worst enemies, besides my controlling, analyzing, intellectualizing, and being compulsive. I told him thanks! and we laughed.

Tonight I really know that I do love Don because he said even though he was on the outside, he walked every step with me while I was becoming unblocked. That said something special because I know I've treated him horribly by throwing tantrums in his office, and he's been the brunt of all my rage, and pain. And yet he stuck by me as I became unblocked and wasn't repelled by all the gory, disgusting, brutalizing things that happened to me. I think the more I pushed him away the more determined he became in sticking around and not leaving me in hopelessness, because he knew how much I needed a man who could accept me. I needed a healthy, warm, caring, gentle male role model because I never had one.

Towards the end of the session, Don made me laugh because he said maybe we'd have 'a burning of the notes' party when the process was over, but I told him no because I need copies of them for my book. He already had my permission to use my letters to help other incest survivors. When I hugged Don good night, our bodies touched and it was OK, no electric shock. It was the first real hug I ever gave Don.

I then went over to Lyn's house and filled her in. I'm so glad she stuck by me, and I didn't let my fear and mistrust keep from letting her in. I love her very much and I'm trying to tell her. I heard a great quote from a man who lost the use of his legs and started studying violin and is a famous violinist. He said 'Separate your abilities from your disabilities.' Right away I thought of my disability of being an incest survivor, but one of my strong abilities is dance. I know that as soon as school is done I will take up dancing.

Wednesday, June 22
• *11:50pm* •

Dear HP

Lyn said the only way I'll be able to have any faith is as I slowly recover and have confidence life. I also shared with her the dreams I've been having about espionage, death, murder, secrecy and the CIA. I'm either the target of death/victim or I'm the observer of the death and torture. I'm doing something wrong in this recovery process because I'm still missing work one or two days a month. The group and Lyn told me to be grateful that I get so much sick time per year and that I'm not fucking up. I feel that way because I'm used to performing at 180 per cent of the time. And that in reality I'm taking care of myself and my needs.

Martha said that in the past I used to shut down whenever I was in touch with my feelings; now that I'm in touch with my feelings, I tend to shut down by becoming physically ill. Don said it's my way of withdrawing from the process. Martha said my physical illnesses are the symptoms of the emotional pain I'm feeling due to incest. That invisible sign 'DON'T COME CLOSE' is not on my chest very often. She said I'd be irresponsible if I didn't rest, take care of myself, and nurture myself. She also said I'm sleeping so much because I'm depressed. I was finally able to hear that I wasn't a fuck-up or irresponsible at work, that I was allowing myself to heal.

Sunday, June 26th
• *11:30pm* •

Dear HP

At a meeting, the person said, 'I'm the one who takes the initiative for the changes in my life so therefore I'm responsible for the changes occurring.' At that moment I realized: even though

I hate this process of recovery, I'm the one who's taking the initiative so that the process of recovery can occur. Three and a half years ago I made a change by going to a recovery program for families of alcoholics, two years ago I made a change by starting therapy, one and a half years ago I made the change by joining a therapy group for adults from alcoholic families, eleven months ago I made the decision to continue therapy when I found out I was an incest survivor, six months ago I made the decision to be part of the incest survivor's group, and in the last two weeks I made the change by letting go of Julie and beginning the mourning process of my child self falling in love with her.

Tonight I realize that it is I who has been making the changes through recovery to face all these issues; therefore, I am responsible for going through the process which is sometimes so horrible. I could have continued to live my life as an emotionally isolated, asexual, over-achiever, but I choose the more painful road of recovery. The other way of life would have been painful and lonely, but I wouldn't have recognized the pain due to my denial. I probably would have been a stressful, compulsive, executive spinster.

Up to now, the recovery process has been hard and painful, and the changes or pluses of recovery have been tiny compared to the pain, and after three and a half years I'm still considered to be in only early stages of recovery.

Thursday, July 7th
● *11:25pm* ●

Dear HP

I shared with Don my realization that I don't believe guys are capable of love and they're only after sex, but since Christopher and Don don't fit into this belief, I needed to make them people with no sex. I also told Don that I didn't view Julie as a female, but a person. I also told him about my beginning to face sexuality issues. Don said until I am able to view him as a man in session the incest will always have power over me. He also said that he thinks that I might have transient homosexual or bisexual feelings but he can't be certain. He said if I were to realize I'm gay it would be all right with him.

I was really honest with him and I told him that I am capable of being emotionally intimate with a woman, but when I fantasize it's always with a man. I said that my feelings for Christopher and Julie were the same, except I realized that I was sexually attracted to Christopher but not to Julie. Don asked me if I wanted to know what part of Christopher I was sexually attracted to. I yelled out 'NO!' and plugged my ears. I told Don I couldn't handle hearing it or facing it in myself right now. Not right now before he goes on vacation for two weeks. We came to the realization that reading *The Joy of Sex* is too advanced for me, that I need to read an updated graphic biology book so I can learn everything about men and women's anatomy and how it works and where it's located. I started to cry at this point, really hard; I realized that my sexuality is so repressed that I never even wanted to read or intellectualize this part of myself.

Saturday, July 30th
● *5:44am* ●

Dear HP

I woke up this morning from a bad dream and I couldn't go back to sleep, so I got up and went out of the house just after 5:00 am this morning to get a pack of cigarettes.

Dreaming

A man comes into the hospital with his hand wrapped up with a plank of wood and bandage. He walks into surgery and he threatens the lives of everyone if they don't bandage him up correctly. The dream has a lot of blood and it ends with me trying to convince my Dad, uncle, and aunt that the man is a bad guy and if they don't believe me, the cops will let him free and he'd come after me.

Monday, August 1st

• *11:14pm* •

Dear HP

First I saw Don on Saturday; and it was great. He made me feel much better by putting things into perspective. I told him about my dreams, and he said if any kid would be able to tell their parent about the incest, I would have. He validated and believed my inner sense. He said even though my father was totally dysfunctional at that time, he would have to live with the guilt if he were to find out the truth today. I realized, therefore, that the incest occurred not only for the two and a half months while my Dad was there. Don said my dreams had a lot of blood, and that I was in 'brown outs' when I had shared memories of blood about my own incest with him. He's certain there was a lot of blood, and that's why it's coming up again.

I was able to share with him about postponing school, hating my job, that this recovery process is like being in the army; putting one foot in front of the other. He said I feel like that because I've made the incest my main vein with work on one side and fun and play on the other. He said I have to start to live again.

Thursday, August 4th

• *11:00pm* •

Don said love is spiritual and relationships are spiritual, and he was in agreement with Lyn (once again). He said I don't have to enmesh myself with incest issues, but I do have to feel the feelings as they come up. I told Don how all I want to do is sleep. I have no words for the pain I'm feeling.

Through Don asking me questions, I came to realize that this pain is shame and it's a big black hole and I feel disgusting and slimy. Don said that shame, disgust and slime are only feelings, and I can heal by peeling one layer of disgust and slime away at the time. I told Don that my child thinks if he sat next to her and held her she might feel better, but there's another voice inside saying, 'Don't be stupid, you don't even like to be held.'

Don sat next to me and I let him hold my finger and cried and he explained how he wouldn't be able to hold someone who was dirty and slimy, but if he had my little girl he would fix her hair and clean her up and straighten out her dress and even put a dab of perfume on her so she would smell good. This really made me cry because I could see him being tender with me as a child. I kept saying it was stupid for me to want him to sit next to me and hold my finger. Don said my child wants to be held and freed from the shame, but my adult is keeping her away because my adult is afraid to take the risk.

I started to cry again because he's right. My adult is scared. I then read my letter to Don telling him about the shame and that I've fallen in love with him. When I realized it, I'd felt joy. He said that was great. After reading my letter I told him I wish that I could slither away under his door as I left. He said only slugs slither, that he doesn't hug slugs. He said when he hugs me he sees a person who is trying to recover. Don also said that if I don't stop trying to control I'll remain a victim of the incest. When I told him I felt stupid about wanting him near me, he said I need to learn how to do that and stop beating myself up. I told Don that my child did trust him; he said that the adult needs to let the child rise above the shame and that on some level I know that he likes me, cares about me, and loves me.

I already knew that, but it was nice to hear. I was crying at one point and Don put his hand under my chin and told me to raise my chin which I did and he turned my head around and told me to open my eyes and look at him. I opened my eyes a slit just to let some light in and them buried my face in my knees. He asked me if he was intrusive and I said yes and he said he was sorry. That really said something to me that Don really respects my limitations and boundaries and would never intentionally cross them. That just made me love him more.

Something as simple and gentle as he did; he was able to apologize for being intrusive. I was able to hug Don goodbye, and I even felt happiness on the way home that I didn't let the feeling of shame control me. My uncle, who crossed all boundaries and was violent, did not have an ounce of sensibility and care that Don has. I think I'm going to learn a lot of positive and beautiful things about men through Don.

Saturday, August 27th

● *3:55am* ●

Dear HP

I believe I'm feeling joy. My little kid is giggling and feels like she got to play hooky. It's been a long day. I slept late and then went to the beach with Antonia, Natalie, and Erica. We then rushed home after a relaxing day and got ready and dressed up to see the play *Les Miserables*. At the beach we'd chatted and I shared about my realization about being a five-and-a-half-year-old emotionally. I came to realize that postponing school and my resistance to changing jobs now that Don said I could were all signs that my inner voice was giving me. Antonia made me realize that I don't have to know the results. All I need to know is the direction and my Higher Power will take care of the rest.

● *4:15pm* ●

Three things are floating in my brain. The play I saw last night, changing jobs, and dealing with sexuality. About the play: it was terrific, moving, sad, and touching. Many people in the theater were crying. There was one scene where Jean Valjean vows to protect and keep Colette, the little girl. He promises her mother on her deathbed to be a guardian for Colette. It brought up my need as a child to be protected, rescued, and saved. And in the middle of this I thought of Don. In the past thirteen months, when I became unblocked and relived the incest and physical abuse, Don in a sense was my protector, because I felt safe enough in therapy to become unblocked. I was also able to see the loving side of a man with a child, and it also reminded me of Don, who has never crossed my boundaries, and who has never rejected me for my rage, and who cared enough to guide me, but also respected my rules and needs while going through this hell. I cried for my little girl who had no one there to protect her and hold her and just wished it had been different, but I was glad and grateful for having Don in my life today.

While in bed this morning, I was fantasizing about having sex and was getting to the point of orgasm, almost over the edge, and I just stopped. It's frustrating, but the worse part is the fear that comes up. It's not so much on a feeling level as it is on a physical level. I tremble from the inside out. Part of me is screaming inside that I shouldn't even be writing about this; it's no one's business but my own. But I believe that feeling is from my child who feels shame and fear. My adult also feels shame because the thought of saying this stuff to Don makes me want to slither away. I just put my hands over my eyes because the shame was so great because of writing this. I remembered the last time I saw Don, that I'd viewed him as a man and had wondered about his penis. I'm definitely not telling Don, but he probably knows anyhow.

I've decided that I'm not doing anything for the next two days until I've read the two chapters in the two anatomy books I have. I did do some reading, but it was getting boring. I felt like I was reading about geology, so I started reading *The Joy of Sex*, and got horny and said to myself let me try masturbating again. I was able to feel some sexual tension but then short circuited. It's the same cycle: horniness, masturbate, short circuit, feeling shame and fear.

Monday, September 6th
● *10:24pm* ●

Dear HP

I've just spoken to Lyn and shared with her my pain of this past weekend, and my need to cry and let go and let her hold me and comfort me. She asked me if I ever saw someone cry and let go. And at first I said no, and then I said yes. Karen really cried and let go at a meeting once and I held her. Lyn told me to call up Karen and ask her how she felt and to call her back and let her know what Karen said, and then Lyn would tell me how she felt the first time she really cried and let go.

I asked Karen. She said she felt really good: she felt like she really let go and she felt comforted. She also said that she was afraid I wouldn't like her any more because the message she got was that if you cried you were a wimp. The first time Lyn cried and someone held her she felt embarrassed at first, but she then felt really comforted, warm, and safe. I guess I needed to know this. Karen cried for a long time, maybe five to ten minutes.

I told Lyn I would pray on my knees for the willingness to let go of the control, that I really need to cry over the loss of my childhood and the physical and sexual abuse, and I need to have her hold me. The need to be comforted and held is becoming greater than the fear. I didn't write in my journal yesterday because I was depressed and isolated. All I did was read the *New York Times* and sleep. I called Lyn, but right before she was about to eat; on some level I knew she wouldn't be available and then she had plans for the evening. I'm glad I spoke with her twice today because earlier I was so shut down that she told me to stop trying to control and to call her tonight. Part of the reason I was so shut down was that Karen made a statement that while she was meditating she felt caressed by God. Just the word caressed shut me down – I know I need to be caressed and held and comforted, but I fear that too much.

Wednesday, September 14th
• *10:20pm* •

Dear HP

I just finished talking to Lyn about shame, and my brain is shutting down on overload. She said I'm stuck in the shame, and the only way to get through the shame is to act as if it's not there when I feel like crying or being held. She said my child's shame is preventing me from being vulnerable. She also asked who's feeling the shame, my adult or my child. I realized it's my child who is feeling the shame because the message in my head is, 'If I had fought harder, none of this would have happened.' On the adult level I know that my child was no physical match for my uncle and that I stopped fighting because I wanted to survive and not die as a result of the physical beatings.

I asked Lyn – since I remembered the physical abuse after the incest does that mean it actually happened that way? She said not necessarily so. She said as I remember more I'll get to know the sequence of events. I know I'm feeling shame because I feel exposed in my clothes, they feel too tight, I want to cut my hair off, I feel ugly and I'm forcing myself to eat at times. I realized that every time I let the shame push people away from me, like feeling distant from Lyn, picking a fight with Don or feeling outside of group, my uncle has the power in my life.

Lyn said as I walk through the shame it will reduce, just like the anger has been reduced compared to last year. The thought of acting as if the shame isn't there makes me nauseous, but I'm going to do it because I want all the power which belongs to me back and I want to bury my uncle. I can't wait to see Don. I feel like I'm on overload. Lyn also made me realize that by closing my eyes when I'm feeling shame I'm pretending it is not there. When my kid is feeling shame she closes her eyes and then puts her right hand over her eyes to make sure she can't see; my child must feel a lot of shame if she has to do that.

HP, give me the willingness to go through the shame because I don't have a clue of what my life would be without it, and I would love to find out.

Friday, September 16th
● *11:59pm* ●

Dear HP

I saw Don tonight; we spoke about shame and he said that my adult is blaming my child, and I realized that I have compassion for other incest survivors or other small children, but not my own. He said that intercourse is not what happened to me as a child. He said intercourse is sex between two consenting people. He said children are not capable of intercourse. He said that I was penetrated by a sick, deranged person, by his genitals, by his penis. By telling my child that intercourse occurred, I'm giving her the message of blame.

I also shared with Don that the shame was affecting my

perception of my clothes and how they fit, and I was feeling very ugly. I also told him how I feel uncomfortable wearing attractive work clothes to see him. By talking about this I came to realize that my adult believes that if she wears attractive clothes she'll get raped or harm will come to her. Don made me realize that the adult is thinking about incest as intercourse, and therefore the belief system in reference to my clothes has to change so that the message of blaming my child can stop. Don also said that by using the shame as a distancer, I'll be able to continue to believe I'm ugly or dirty or slimy and it helps me to keep myself invisible. He told me to stop eating what I'm not supposed to so I don't shut down my feelings. I have the choice to let my child run my life like I have the past two days or change the messages of my adult, comfort my child and continue to go through the shame.

As of Saturday morning I'm going back to no sugar or yeast. When I told Don my dream about the torn wedding gown, he said it represents my fear of emotional exposure.

Higher Power, I'm afraid to feel visible. The one good analogy I came up with was that there are gorgeous models who look not only attractive but beautiful, and they're not attacked and killed, or raped and beaten just because they're so attractive. So, I'm going to act as if and try to look attractive and not eat sugar and yeast and talk to my child with my new awareness. Higher Power, give me the strength, willingness, and courage to move forward instead of slipping back. Lyn was right. I'm blaming my child.

Tuesday, September 20th.

● *2:55pm* ●

Dear HP

I promised Lyn that I would write down whenever I woke in the middle of the night so here's my dream recopied from a note pad at the side of my bed at 2:38 am.

Dreaming

I'm in a full length slip about to be examined by a doctor and all I feel is terror. I'm so terrified that I can't even remove my slip. The next scene has to do with limestone and gravel. It's too close to my back and I break out in a cold sweat and finally the last part of the dream is that I'm married to an oriental man who needs to be married to me for another twenty-five hours more and then he'll be legal.

I had another dream that I remembered when I woke up this morning.

Dreaming

We were in Maine and Andria, my cousin who recently got married, comes running down the hill to tell me she's pregnant after being married a month. I think to myself in disgust, 'Couldn't they have some self control and use some protection at least?' I think – great! Andria is fucked up and now she's going to bring another human being into the world who will be as fucked up as her mother. I just walk away feeling angry and disgusted with my cousin.

In this dream at least I know I'm projecting my own feelings onto Andria. I would love to someday have a child, but a big part of me feels so fucked up due to the incest that I wouldn't even dream of bringing a child into my world until my head was screwed on right. Most women my age (27) and older start wanting to have children. I'm still trying to overcome with Lyn and Don the terror I feel so I can be comforted and nurtured. On some level I know I would be good with kids and yet never have any of my own. Who knows?

Sunday September 25th

• *2:42am* •

Dear HP

I also told Don about the dream I had on Tuesday. Don said being in a slip represented a gynecological visit (which I had last month), he said the limestone and the gravel had to do with the incest and that it could have occurred outdoors. The marriage represented the feeling that I believe I'll just be used again, and the dream of Andria was really my feelings about myself. I had the following dream on Thursday at 2:32 am and woke up in terror:

Dreaming

It's in the gulf of Mexico and there's an executive and his child swimming in the water. The executive drowns while saving his own child from a whirlpool. The whirlpool becomes a hole and just swallows up the executive. The child was eight years old when saved and today at sixteen or seventeen is a heroine addict.

Don said the child was me who was saved even with the abuse, but still turned out to be diseased by being an incest survivor. Don said he might represent the executive but he wasn't sure. Don was surprised at the hopelessness and said that I can change the present and future by walking the walk. It was really funny and cute seeing Don laugh so hard that he couldn't catch his breath and was crying.

Tonight I went to a dinner party at Gena's house and it was amazing. First of all I looked attractive; I really tried and it was so strange, I got complimented on my hair, my clothes, even my make-up. I can't believe people notice such things. In addition, I knew at least for tonight that I wasn't boring. We talked about hunting, waxing off hair, food, books, funny stories, etc. I felt really comfortable and at ease. I met and spent some time with Antonia's boyfriend. It was really nice seeing Antonia with him. It gave me a lot of hope because in some ways Antonia is like me, and I hope that Don is right and that I'll begin to date in a couple of months. Seeing Antonia with her boyfriend almost made me want to be going out with someone. I just saw a lot of care, love, and flirting which was adorable.

Monday, September 26th

● *3:15am* ●

Dreaming

I'm in a line in gym waiting to take ID pictures. Then I go up spiral stairs to lockers, and one black kid starts pushing people and the white kid who is the captain of a team talks to him; the black kid pokes him in the eye. The white kid almost punches him; instead he walks over and talks to our union president. Then my Dad's best friend and myself are in front of a display at a store talking. My mother comes over and then his wife, except she's another woman and he walks away from her and goes far away to read a bestseller book. I'm far away, but I can see what he's reading. It's about a husband, wife, and little child. The jacket of the book says how the man missed the child tugging at his hair, the smell of baby and so forth; so he kills the wife to have the child all to himself. The book begins with the wife and husband newly married, at a grave site with a grave digger with white wild hair. The book jumps to the present where they're both at a cemetery; because he tried to kill the wife, the child died. They're talking and while they're talking the wife pulls out a small gun and shoots the husband dead. All of a sudden the husband jumps up and kills her and her boyfriend even though he's wounded and bleeding. I'm watching this all from a far away place. The next scene (which was the worst and woke me up shaking), is in a long hallway. There is this man who shot his wife and hundreds of other men who have holes in their bodies and are bleeding all over. I'm walking through in shock, terror, and disgust. I wind up in a corner between two men who are in agony. One turns to me and gives me a bag with several million dollars and says to me, 'Return it all. This money is doing me no good. The worst way to die is to have holes in you and bleed. Look at my son.' (The son was on the other bed next to

*him). Then the son sits up and screams, 'Don't take the money,
it belongs to me. My father says he never touched me. That's true
except he ate my hand.' And all I see is a bloody wrist.*

(That's when I woke up shaking.)

September 28th

● 3:00am ●

Dreaming

*I'm leaving work to go home, and I see my boss who is at the
table drinking and says hi to me and laughs. I just walk away.
I'm so confused I walk to the wrong parking lot. Then I'm
waiting for a bus, and a riot begins and some woman helps me
and saves me, and a whole bunch of people go to this house.
They're really strange and all I want to do is leave, and she
says if I cause trouble she's going to tell everyone that I have
underwear with fish on them. I leave this house when this guy
who looks like Howard comes to visit. Meanwhile, I'm with my
car mechanic who I trust and he tells me that all I need is a
14" screw for my air filter. Someone had put in a wrong size
screw.*

*He then tells me that I need to find a nice guy who knows
about my car and can take care of my bronchitis. Next, I'm
walking and Howard is cutting grass and trees with a pizza
cutter and he's trying to cut me up. Then all of a sudden
Howard becomes a little kid and starts cutting open his chest.
At first no blood comes out, and he starts walking and says he
can't feel anything because he grew up in an alcoholic family.
The next scene is the little kid's chest all cut up and he's lying
in a pool of blood with his little shoes lined up next to him.
A man has passed out next to him. In the next scene, the same
little kid is wrapped up in a blanket, and his mother is holding
him and kissing him and there's a doctor checking out Howard.
The man is alive and also being checked out. He had had a*

stroke when he saw his kid was all cut up. Then the father crawls over to the mother, and kid and all three snuggle together. The kid looks up at the doctor and says, 'I'm glad I didn't die and now I can feel my skin so I won't hurt myself.' And the doctor laughs and says 'Great, go play in the afternoon sun and join a little league.'

● *11:31pm* ●

I hate this fucking process. I saw Don tonight and more memories are coming up as a result of the two dreams I had this week. I remembered that there use to be an underground tunnel about two houses away from my grandparents in Italy; it went from one side of the street to the other. As a result of talking to Don about my dreams, I'm afraid to remember what happened in the tunnel. In my dreams there have been two tunnels where there's blood and water on the ground.

Tonight I asked Don if the blood came from the incest or physical abuse; he said the incest. For some reason when he said that I shivered. I said, 'Don, I only bled one time, which was the first time.' He said no, that it's not like some women are who bleed when they lose their virginity. So I came to realize that every time I was raped there was probably blood, and Don said maybe even torn tissues. I started gagging right in Don's office. I also realized that I almost died in that tunnel; it was on the wall in the tunnel that I got my head bashed in. I just started crying.

Lyn says it's good that the memories are coming up and out; they'll take up less room in my head. I feel like it's five steps forward and eight back. Don said I was not to obsess about this, and to write down any dream I have in the morning. I was in so much pain that I drove over to Lyn's house and cried with her a little bit. I felt so sad, and pained for my little girl. I hope that just as I've had much pain and abuse as a child from a man, I will have that much love and comfort from a man too. I'm very afraid to look in that underground tunnel; it holds a lot of pain, blood, terror, and brutality.

I do have to add that even though the nightmares have been back this week, I haven't missed work and am actually having fun and even went out last night during the week. I hope I can handle anything that comes up.

Saturday, October 8th
● 1:12am ●

I almost forgot! I had a big breakthrough in therapy with Don. He was so happy that he threw the armrest slip covers and his Velamints in the air. Sometimes, he's so cute! I was telling Don that by remembering the blood and reading the anatomy books about the various sizes of vagina and urinary openings, and then downgrading them to a five-and-a half-year-old's body, and comparing them to how big my uncle's penis must have been, all of a sudden I felt pain and sadness.

I really believed that just maybe my little girl didn't cause the incest nor want it to happen, because of how painful and bloody it must have been. Don said he's known all along that it wasn't my fault, but I had to emotionally believe that and that I just punched my first fist through the wall of guilt and shame. I asked him if that was good and he said that was great.

Friday, October 14th
● 10:21pm ●

Dear HP

So much has happened that I haven't had any time to write. On Tuesday, I didn't have group but went to an Elton John concert. It was great, but I was also sad because I was beginning to feel a loss over my adolescent years. On Wednesday, I chaired a meeting and the topic was trusting, and I was able to realize I'm not trusting myself, my recovery, Lyn, or Don.

When I spoke to Lyn about it, she helped me so much. I told her that, now that I've closed the door on the past, I feel like I've been thrown out in the world and told deal with my life without having a clue how to begin. All I'm feeling is fear, anxiety and overwhelmed. Lyn said that all I have to do is trust her and Don, as I've been trying to do, and everything else will fall in place. She also said that I've been through the worst of this process and it's scary but not like last year.

I was able to tell her that somehow through this process my child is not five-and-a-half, but now is eleven or twelve and beginning adolescence. I also told her that I'm noticing guys a lot. She said that's OK and maybe I'm feeling shame over these new feelings. I felt so much better talking to her.

On Thursday when I saw Don we had a really good session. I was able to tell him how much I do love him and care for him, that it's no longer acceptable for me to get angry at him as a defense. I told him I trust him as much as it's possible for me to trust a man today. I realize that emotionally I trust him completely, and it's his maleness that I'm having a hard time trusting. Don made me realize that I hadn't once looked at him throughout the session. All of a sudden this huge pain came up; I realized that by me telling Don my feelings for him he would reject me, think I was stupid and ugly and just gag at the thought of me being near him. I'm so afraid of seeing all this in his face that I don't look at him at all.

Don said that my body image is still off and if I looked up at him I'd see for myself what he thought. It was so scary that I couldn't do it nor even breathe. Don said, if I looked down my uncle would win because of the effect the incest has had in my life, and if I looked up my uncle would lose because Don would not hurt or reject me or abuse my love for him like my uncle did. When Don told me to look up, the only reason why I had the willingness to look at his face three separate times in the session was because I didn't want my uncle to win. Each time I looked up and saw Don's face, all I saw was warmth, love, and acceptance of what I had just told him. Even when I hugged him goodnight he wasn't grossed out by me. It was I who hugged him like I was cardboard once again.

I've come to realize, with Don's help, that I'm mourning my adolescence and mourning the fact that I wasn't part of it. I also mourn the fact that there were many nice, special guys while I was growing up, and yet I wasn't able to feel safe or see their beauty – as a result of the incest. Part of me wants to be out all night, buy records, and clothes, and giggle and experiment with make-up and check out guys. I still can't get over how my thoughts about guys are changing so much. Don said just let it continue.

Sunday, October 23rd
● *10:50pm* ●

Dear HP

Right now I'm feeling sad. There's so many feelings of love that I want to express to Don and Lyn, and the intensity scares me as well as my fear of rejection. I feel comfortable and safe with Lyn, and yet when I get to the point of sharing some of the things I needed from my mom, all this pain and hurt comes up. I was able to cry, but I just wasn't able to reach out and ask Lyn to hold me. She said that maybe I need to accept where I am.

I love Lyn emotionally so very much and yet I'm so afraid to combine the physical nurturing aspect to it. I do know that if I can't let Lyn hold me, I'll never be able to let any man hold me. Yesterday, my mother mentioned that she thought one of my aunts and uncles was an incest survivor, and yet I'd thought that a different aunt was an incest survivor. Suddenly, I realized that the perpetrator was probably my grandfather, and out of ten kids he probably incested four that I'm almost positive about. I realized that he was also physically and verbally abusive towards my grandmother, who herself was an incest survivor. I've no proof, nor will I ever have, but all of a sudden I know this to be true. And it's really weird, but Lyn said she had thought for a long time that my uncle was my grandfather re-incarnated.

Tuesday, November 8th
● *11:42pm* ●

Tonight, my Dad spoke to me and he said he wanted to know what happened to me that was so bad over this past year or so. I told him that I've chosen not to deal with it on a family level (I didn't tell him that Mom knew about the incest) because it would hurt him too much. I told him I am getting help through individual and group counseling. He said that by me not telling him, he won't be able to come to me when he needs help. I told him I hope that he would go to his wife before he came to speak to his daughter. He asked me what if he could only talk to me; he wouldn't be able to talk to me because I wouldn't tell him about my past year or so. I told him that he wouldn't come to me because he had made that decision.

I also encouraged my father to look on the positive side; how much more attractive I look, that I'm feeling a lot better, that I'm more intimate with my family than ever before. He kind of disregarded this and was only able to see the pain I was in. He also told me that I would get into trouble, because I didn't believe in 'God', meaning Catholicism. I was able to thank him for his love and concern, and tell him to stop trying to pry, because he wasn't getting an answer from me, but that didn't mean I loved him less.

I also spoke with Martha, the group therapist. She said I would have to desensitize myself by being touched. For a while it will be painful, but I need to tell myself that I'm here, that it's OK to be touched by this person and I want to be in this time and space. Tonight in group I was able to hear different members speak about their relationships, and was able to hear that they're not as healthy as I thought they were. Also, there is one person in my group who doesn't have a boyfriend and is dating and doesn't want to be touched. I felt a little bit better talking to Martha. Stacey and I are going on a shopping spree to buy new clothes, next Saturday. I can't wait.

Sunday, November 20th
- 10:30pm -

Today was the first day I exercised at the health club. It felt great. I'm suffering backlash. Yesterday, Stacey and I spent all day shopping and I have some really nice outfits. I'm having an anxiety attack because the clothes I bought are attractive and I like them and I needed them; by spending so much money on myself and wearing the clothes, I'm beginning to break the myth of how ugly I am.

Today, I had a realization and I know it's the truth for me. I realize that I'll probably not be going to graduate school for some time because I can hide in school; I can hide behind my intellect and bury my feelings, so I realize school is out. I think the process will slowly reveal to me as to which direction I'll be going in reference to work. Maybe I'm projecting, but I get the sense of changing my job in the next six months. Only time will tell.

Sunday, December 11th
● *9:40pm* ●

Dear HP

Friday, I finally got my car back. I'm free! I saw Don on Friday night and I came to realize that when Carmen was describing how I spoke about Don in group, it was a shock to me because it was the first time that I consciously put the whole picture together; not only did I love Don, but I was in love with him, and I was sexually attracted to him. Don said that the only reason I was able to finally admit it now is that before it was too close and too overwhelming. Don wanted me to start talking to him about my feelings, but it was so difficult. I told him that I keep shutting down like there was a short in a wire. He said that I keep shutting down due to my control and that all the wires are working if only I would let them.

Yesterday was a great day. I felt gratitude and joy. I spent the day in the city Christmas shopping, went to look at the decorated store windows and the Rockerfeller Center. Today was good, too. I did chores like laundry and food shopping. I also called Karen to tell her that I was sorry for shutting down when she needed me most, that I needed some space so I could try to undo this triangle and not continue hurting her while I try to sort out my anger and fear towards her. I realize that Karen triggers issues of intimacy, faith, and sexuality. After talking to Karen, I felt like a worm and called Lyn. I realize that Karen has very strong needs and they aren't expressed verbally but through her actions, and I feel smothered. I also feel that she had crossed my boundaries. I realized, for me because she's gay she represents a man to me, and I felt scared. I had to tell myself that she's a woman and that it's OK.

1989

January 4th
● *9:30pm* ●

Dear HP

I took out the passport photo of when I was five and a half. Now I know why my eyes were so sad; I felt those feelings of being sent away. Today, I wanted to flick that picture in my mother's face and say to her, 'You fucked up, and you have helped in fucking up my whole life by sending me there, but more so by not noticing any difference when I came home.' Part of me wants to grill my mother as to why I was sent there and another part of me wants to shake her until her teeth rattle. I'm angry at perpetrators again.

Two women in group are going to see their perpetrators this week, and I shared in group that this flash went through me of cracking a bottle and slicing the perpetrator up with it. A pretty violent and bloody thought.

I called my mom to cancel dinner plans on Friday. I told her I need some space because I'm dealing with past family issues, and when I'm around them I shut down because my relationship with her today is different than that of the child. What I really wanted to tell her is that I'm paying for her fucked-up mistake of sending a five-and-a-half-year-old away.

Saturday, January 8th
● *12:40am* ●

Dear HP

I saw Don on Thursday and I realized that I want him to be with me when I deal with this stuff with my Mom. Don said I need to get a photograph of my child that is joy filled prior to the incest. Don carries a picture of himself as a small boy. He said that the picture of me from my passport is a picture of a heartbroken little girl. I'm really pissed at my Mom, she really fucked up by sending me to Italy and yet a part of me knows she was desperate.

Talking to Lyn last night made me realize why the pain surfaces when I hear her voice. Lyn has been there for my child through all the awkwardness of new relationships, throughout the pain, terror, and rage of the incest and through all the phases up to now in dealing with intimacy. But when I look back as a child, I realize how alone I really was. It was just a very painful and lonely childhood. Lyn has been there for me emotionally more so than my mother has ever been. Don suggests that eventually I bring my Mom into counseling so that some healing can take place.

Thursday, January 26
● *10:17pm* ●

Dear HP

I'm doing so much better now that I saw Don. I realized that I was angry and sad with Don. I was angry with Don because I misunderstood him. Don was trying to imply that eventually the incest won't have the physical power over me. I heard that I will have no flashbacks now that I've closed the door. I was also sad that the feeling of being in love and feeling safe with Don could not be as easy in real life. Don said that the physical aspect makes it harder and that there are differences between the therapeutic relationship and dating outside, but that a therapeutic relationship does mirror a real intimate relationship in some ways.

Sunday, January 29th
● *12:15am* ●

Dear HP

I had a great day. I bought four CDs, and went to see *Beaches* with Stacey and her friend Dori. Then we went back to Stacey's and hung out. The movie made me cry. I identified with the little girl who lost her mother; she had CC, her Mom's best friend, to go to. I realized that there was no one there for me during the incest and when I realized that my Mom couldn't be there, I stopped wanting or missing her. I just shut down. I ache with the feeling of realizing that as a five-and-a-half-year-old I was totally alone and emotionally dependant upon myself.

Today, I'm learning how to need people like Lyn and Don. I feel very sad for my inner child. I lost it for fifteen seconds, and I sobbed for that small child. She was so shut down that she couldn't even be held.

I've been feeling a spiritual loss and sadness and I need to talk about feeling betrayed by the Catholic Church and hiding within the church to deny my sexuality. I need to be at peace so I can go on and begin some kind of spiritual journey. Right now the only spiritual journey I'm doing is trusting the process, as well as Lyn and Don. The words in the song *Landslide* bring up my feelings about my mother.

Something cracked inside me. I have just finished sobbing on the phone with Lyn. I called her at 11.30 pm. My kid thinks she was sent away because she's unlovable and my uncle only confirmed that. Lyn said that wasn't really why I was sent away, but my adult can't even fight that because she thinks she's unlovable too.

I got off the phone with Lyn, and I realize that the intimate feelings I buried are somehow connected to my femininity. Today I'm told I look feminine on the outside but, as Lyn said, all I have to do is shake in terror for two minutes and she knows the insides don't match the outside. By going through this process, I'll eventually be able to express intimate feelings to those I care about, as well as feel intimate.

What I needed from you, Mom, as a child:

- I needed you to not have sent me away.

- I needed you to tell me I was warm and loving, and an adorable kid.

- I needed you to tell me it was great being a little girl.

- I needed you to tell me it was OK for me to express my love.

- I needed you to see that I wasn't the same kid that left.

- I needed you to protect me from Uncle Marco.

- I needed you to hold me and make me feel safe.

- I needed you to acknowledge what had happened and tell me it wasn't my fault, that I wasn't ugly and slimy.

- I needed you to walk right through my defenses, scoop me up, and get some help for me.

- I needed to get angry at you for sending me away and not being there to protect me.

- I needed to know that I wasn't sent away because I was unlovable.

- I needed to have mattered to you.

What I need from you, Mom, today:

- to make amends to me.

- to trust you.

- to have your love and respect.

- to like the woman I'm becoming.

- to accept me as a smart, attractive woman.

- to give me permission to express myself.

- to be affectionate towards me and to help me become that way too.

Today, I'm feeling rage – probably towards my mother but it's really not directed. I feel that everything is a big fucking deal because I don't have a clue about needs, comforting, affection, or anything to do with intimacy. I feel gypped. I feel betrayed by my mother because my uncle stole my innocence and tenderness, and my mother had dealt with me as if nothing had changed. She continues to allow my uncle to steal that intimacy by not noticing any difference in me. So today at twenty-eight years old I hesitate and resist getting my needs met – because I don't know what they are, and because I'm uncomfortable if they get met. I'm afraid to ask in case I'm rejected.

Friday June 9th

I'm so angry at my father. He's playing the role of the fucking wimp. I stopped by and I just felt so uncomfortable anywhere near him, so in turn I feel uncomfortable with everyone. I really hate my father; he's twenty-two years too late. I can just see him falling apart when I tell him my story; he'll want comforting. I have still not been able to cry. I feel like a rocket about to take off, but whether I'll cry and beat the shit out of someone is hard to tell.

I've just polished off four small bran muffins. I needed to do something defiant and I was hungry. They had no sugar or yeast. I feel like some part of my insides is finally cracking and this loathing and rage are finally coming out. Part of me would like to raise hell and really give it to my father, and another part of me doesn't care at all about him, and then there's that little girl who was rejected and betrayed by her father.

Sunday, June 11th

● *1:56pm* ●

Just came in from spending the evening with Gena. We went to the Village, walked around and got to go to Tower Records, a first, it was great. I bought a pair of earrings, a small Batman button, and an amethyst stone. Amethyst, I believe, represents healing and peace. We went for coffee at an outside cafe. It was so NYC-ish – I love it. Today I spent a good bit of money on myself. I bought a self-waxing kit for my lips and eyebrows. It was really funny. It took three and a half hours plus two lip burn marks and wax over everything; but I no longer have hairy lips or eyebrows. I just hope the burn marks go away soon. It will be worth it once I get the hang of it, but it was really a lot of fun. I'm beginning to realize that I can still have fun and be tearful or in pain. I had a super excellent day. I'm really glad I'm getting to know Gena. She's so childlike, yet so wise. I hope tomorrow is as beautiful and sunny as planned so Stacey and I can have a great day.

• 11:21pm •

Had another great day. I got to spend the morning by myself, relaxing eating breakfast, reading the *New York Times*. Then Stacey and I went to the beach. I got sunburned. It was very relaxing, and fun. I came home, ate dinner, and went to Stuart's home to celebrate Antonia's birthday and again it was a lot of fun. Not only were Antonia, Gena, Erica, and Natalie there, but there were also other people. We got to laugh and tell funny stories.

Right now there's a very happy person writing this and yet my eyes have tears. I'm beginning to really understand that I can live my life, and yet at times I feel depressed, sad, and angry as stuff comes up. I know crap about my Dad is leaking out – I was angry and tearful on Friday, Saturday night for a little bit, and tonight too, and yet it hasn't stopped me from having a wonderful weekend.

Thursday, June 14

• 12:41am •

I've decided to write because I can't sleep. My kid is racing around in my stomach and thoughts are racing in my head. I've asked my sisters to come over on Tuesday evening at 9.00 so that I can tell them about the incest and make amends. Part of me is scared (actually terrified) and part of me is excited. I'm scared of the secret, and am afraid of not being believed. I'm afraid I'll be rejected or my pain will be minimized. I'm afraid they won't understand why I'm making amends. I'm excited because somehow my little girl is going to get the chance to meet their little girls again. I'm afraid of making myself vulnerable to them. I haven't done it for a very long time. I'm also trying to be part of a family I quitted emotionally twenty-two years ago, while realizing that they're not in recovery and my relationship with them is limited. Even though I wanted to do this for a long time, I'm afraid to take the risk but I know it's time.

Sunday June 18th

● *11:00pm* ●

I was able to tell my father that I wasn't coming over for Father's Day because I have too much anger towards him. He wanted to know if it was about the present or the past, and did he do something, and did the reason I didn't believe in God any more have anything to do with it? I told him there were several people involved, and it had to do with how he handled a situation and that once I had walked through this anger I would talk to him.

I told him I'd already spoken with Mom, and I was talking to Annamarie and Vanessa next, and then Lino, and him last. He expected the fact that he was last that I was going to judge him and he was going to be on trial. He told me he wanted someone there when I told him. I told him I was sharing my story, and he couldn't tell me how to do it.

He asked me was it fact, or was it my feelings because I'd thought all those years that he had just left me in Italy by myself. I told him that I didn't spend two nights a week for the past three years driving sixty miles just because of my feelings or perceptions. I didn't lose fifteen pounds because of feelings. I didn't become suicidal because of my feelings. I didn't go on an anti-depressant because of my feelings. All of it is based on facts. He said nothing that bad had happened to me. I wasn't abused. Not once did I use that word with him. I told him he didn't know what he was talking about so just be quiet.

I realize that my Dad is probably afraid of being judged. I just wished he had handled me differently twenty-two years ago. I broke down and started to cry. My heart is breaking for that little girl. I'd never once used the word 'abuse' with him, and my Dad saying I wasn't abused just broke my denial some more and reconfirmed my inner feeling. I know that I had told him everything, that he didn't do anything.

Dear Dad

I have no memory of you, Dad, because you weren't there to protect me. I needed protection because my life was at stake.

Your presence really didn't count because you really weren't there to protect me, and once I told you, you weren't there to believe me. And you haven't been there for me since I told you – you chose to bury the secret with Uncle Marco's death and I choose to bury you with Uncle Marco. You betrayed me by not doing anything, and I realized that Uncle Marco was right. No one would believe me.

Dad, many people believe me today. Don, a total stranger three years ago believed in me enough to take me on as a client. He's believed every part of my story and never has he made me feel untouchable, unlovable, or a misfit. He has had more acceptance of me in three years than you've had of me my whole life.

Dad, on one hand you'd say I have nothing to be ashamed of, and on the other you were critical and judgmental. Dad, I'm the thorn in your side – defiant, opinionated, and determined. I'm a constant reminder that you're a fuck-up, so instead of owning that, you tried to put it on me. I'm a constant reminder of the very good chance that there was incest in your own family. I'm a constant reminder of everything you've got drunk over. Dad, if it was up to you, I'd be the ugly, determined hardworking spinster who lived at home with you until you dropped.

Dad, I'm going to shatter your denial for my own benefit. No, you do not know me better that I know myself. That's just your ego, and grandiosity speaking. I'm breaking the denial because I'm not going to let the secret be buried with your brother. The one good part of that is – everyone in my immediate family will know what a disgusting prick Uncle Marco was; his canonization by his family, and my shame, can finally be blown apart. I'm not willing to keep the secret any longer.

Incest is a part of who I am, whether you like it or not. I really don't care what you think of me because my opinion of you is so low, your opinion of me is worthless. You have no power over me, you don't care about me, and I have a lot less to lose than you do. You still need to believe in your grandiosity as a father and your all-knowing wisdom. Well, it's a crock of shit. Just like your brother Marco was to this wonderful kid who died.

Saturday, June 24th
• *12:56am* •

Had a great evening. I got my hair cut tonight and it looks great! I love it. Then Erica, Christopher, Carol his wife, and myself went out to dinner at a great Mexican restaurant. It was good seeing them. Carol was really funny. They want to adopt a child from Latin America. I could really see them doing that. It was good to hear that they're dealing with transitions and are able to work things out. They give me a lot of hope.

Tuesday, June 27th
• *9:00pm* •

Dear Dad

You have milked every drop out of your manic depression that is possible in order to absolve yourself of your actions. You wore being an undiagnosed manic depressive for sixteen years as a badge of courage and honor. People should admire, acknowledge and emulate you for the simple fact that you didn't kill yourself and you supported a family throughout those years.

Dad, let me burst your bubble of denial very quickly. You can take all your martyrdom and shove it up your ass. You didn't commit suicide, but there where many times I wished you had died, and Annamarie shared those feelings too. You used your manic depression to cop out on life, to promote your alcoholism, and to shirk off anything you might have done wrong, saying you did the best you could. Dad, your best I could do without. It stinks; there is no best, and it only feeds your ego and denial. The fact is that you did not believe me, validate me, protect me or nurture me in any aspect of being an incest survivor at the age of five and a half.

Dad, my rage at you is about dealing with my reality, and shattering your imposed image of how great a father you were. To the rest of the family maybe you were a good father, to some degree; they're younger and lived through fewer years in your insanity. As for myself, you are not getting a break. Dad, you destroyed a five-and-a-half-year-old, a victimized and brutalized little girl, by not believing her story, by not comforting her, and by idolizing her perpetrator. Dad, twenty-two years of my life have been fucked up because you did nothing. By denying everything I said, you condoned all your brother's actions. Dad, I've so much hatred and rage towards you that I am almost not able to feel it. The sad part is that proportionate to feeling rage and hatred is feeling hurt, betrayal, and devastation.

I pray you die before Mom, and suddenly, because I'm not willing to parent and nurture you as you get older. Explain to me how you can make up for twenty-two years of my life. For all the horrible feelings of being an incest survivor, I have you to blame. Dad, you did nothing for twenty-two years, and those horrible feelings grew, fermented, and seeped into every cell; I thought I was unlovable, untouchable, ugly, disgusting, asexual, stupid and a disgusting slug. You allowed twenty-two years of hell to continue just because you needed to keep a secret, just because you couldn't deal with reality.

Dad, you're such a fucking, spineless wimp. It was my nightmare, my reality, my body, my soul, that was tortured and you, being a stupid fuck, couldn't even deal with it. You'd better pray that you don't have to depend on me because I don't know if I'll be able to come through. I hate you so much, I don't even want recovery for you. I just want you to disappear, so I can have my family to myself.

Thursday, June 29th
● 6:35pm ●

So much has happened. Yesterday morning I was still angry and I didn't want to see my Dad. By yesterday afternoon they had ruled out an aneurysm and a stroke, although the CAT scan showed an abnormality. I started to laugh and my eyes began to leak. When I shared this with Molly, she told me that it was OK to feel angry and I need not feel guilty over my feelings. When I spoke to her later, she reminded me that feelings change and I was not to let my family pressure me.

I called Don and he said a day or two of not seeing my

father would be OK since they were still testing, but eventually I would want to come to peace with him and see him, because to not do so would eventually hurt me. Don gave me permission to change my feelings.

Last night at 7:00 I was taking Vanessa to the doctor because she had the flu. Annamarie called; the doctors had found a tumor and they were operating this morning and Dad was asking for me. At that moment I knew I had to see him. I knew I loved him, I was just so angry.

When I got to the hospital, I told him he didn't have to go into the hospital to get off my shit list. My Dad's face was drooping on one side and he looked scared. We took a break downstairs and I started to cry because I realized I do love him and he does matter, I was just so angry. I went upstairs crying and talked to my Dad. I told him he tried to be the best father he could, but I still had to stay away to work through the feelings. He said he was not responsible for other people's behavior, that God gave each of us a free will. I told him he could believe anything he wanted to if it worked for him, but I was working on a new higher power. He told me he worked so very hard not be like his father and he felt he had succeeded. He said he really tried to be the best parent he could be and he's sorry if I got hurt, but he really tried.

While we were there, his heart monitor rose and we thought nothing of it. After Annamarie and I went home, Mom came home and let us know that the surgery to remove the tumor had been postponed until Friday morning. Annamarie and I got to talk; she said she wasn't angry that I'd stayed away but she was worried. She said I had enough to deal with about Dad and the incest, and she didn't want something to happen to Dad and I would regret not making peace with him. I forgot, Dad made me promise that I would talk to him (about the incest when I was ready).

This morning I went to work because I didn't want to wait in a hospital or at home, and I needed a familiar environment. At 9:00 am when I arrived at work there was a message on my desk from Vanessa. All Vanessa told me was that at 8:15 this morning they decided to operate because the pressure in Dad's brain kept increasing. I walked into my boss's office and told him my Dad was being operated on and my voice cracked. I had been preparing myself for surgery on Friday, not today. Mom asked me to be at the hospital between 11:30 and noon when Dad got out of surgery. At 2:30 pm the doctor came out and told us he had removed almost all of the tumor, and the other two per cent was surrounding the motor control and Dad would have been paralyzed if it had been removed. The tumor was a brain tumor and it was malignant. The small part left in the brain would continue to grow. Dad would be in the hospital for a week and then start chemotherapy.

Monday, July 3rd
• *8:10pm* •

Went to work today. I was able to get a lot done and yet I was tearful. I feel so betrayed by my father because I now know I told him about the incest when my uncle died.

Tuesday, July 4th
• *11:38pm* •

Dad

I decided to write this since I probably couldn't ever tell you. I hate your fucking family, and I hate many aspects of being half Italian. I hate your family because of their arrogance, their lack of boundaries, and their superior attitude. Of nine of your siblings, I care about three of them and their families. I hate the rest of them due to their narrowmindedness, the dysfunctions that are in the form of alcoholism, over-eating, controlling attitudes, verbal, physical, emotional, and sexual abuse. I hate their skin, hair, and eye coloring. I hate their accents. Your family for the most part are all dicks, and I'm disowning them. Dad, when you die I will have absolutely nothing to do with most of them. I hate their pettiness, selfishness, and how many were parasites sucking both you and Mom dry; and you let them. Only now are you realizing it. If you should decide to be buried in Italy that will truly be the end. I hate your country and your family. I will never be attracted to someone with black/brown hair, olive skin and brown eyes. Dad, thank God you only have the dark hair because I wouldn't have been able to stand olive skin as well.

Dad, the reality is that it's easier to hate your family right now than to hate you. I keep splitting – my little girl is buried alive somewhere because it's not safe to be around my immediate family or your fucking family. Dad, by getting sick once again you are affecting my life. The reality is Dad that there's a little girl who loved you a long time ago, but she's been buried for years. My adult doesn't know you, like you or respect you; and yet, part of me loves you and a part of me hates you.

Dad, I'm back to having my life out of control because of your disease. Dad, my life is back on hold. I can't change jobs when all I want to do is cry. I don't even know what I want to do. It makes it hard to find out when I know you're dying and there are fine people that I love very much who are hurting too. I just wish you would die already, or recover from your diseases. You are fucking up my life again. I feel like I'm in a spider's web and I can't get out. I just want my life back, preferably without your involvement in it because you have never been any help.

Dad, I love you, but I hate what you did to me, how you treated me and I don't need you now. You are twenty-two fucking years too late. I don't want to put my life on hold and I need help so I can get out of the spider's web again. Dad, I love you – that is, my child did – my adult hates you. Truthfully, I hope you die by the end of the summer or the chemo and radiation kills the tumor and then I can bow out of the picture. Dad I want to change jobs, date, have fun, but I can't because you are once again a fucking ball and chain around my neck. I hope the rest of this rage comes out so I can stop abusing my body and myself.

Saturday, July 8th
● *12:05am* ●

I went over to my parents' house for dinner and I told my father I would talk to him later in the afternoon. My father said,

'Talk to me now or don't talk to me at all because I don't have tomorrow.' So, we both went into the bedroom. I asked my Higher Power for guidance and I told my father everything. He asked me if I was raped and I said many times. He said that I never told him about the incest as a child and that he is not so cold-hearted that he would not have responded. He said that he wished I'd told him earlier so that we would have more time together, because he believes he's going to die within two weeks. I told him that up to two weeks ago I was protecting him because he loved Uncle Marco.

He said, 'You don't protect ugliness, you protect beauty like you Yvette.' He said he always knew I loved him but that I couldn't express it, and considering what happened to me I could have turned into an animal, but I didn't. He said he never thought I was ugly, that my uncle was a bastard. He told me he knew I was in love with Christopher, and there are a lot of nice guys out there like Christopher. They're not all bastards, but I have to give them a chance. He said he was so sorry and thanked God that Uncle Marco had died because he would have flown over and killed him since now he has nothing to lose.

He said Uncle Marco is dead and died a long time ago. I'm his daughter and I'm alive. He also said I must make sure I get some faith – even if it's a different religion. I told him that there is a little girl who really does love him and I sobbed in his arms twice. I cried for both of us. I was crying really hard because the wound was open, my father said, 'That's enough, Yvette,' and I stopped crying on the spot. At least my father understands why I was the way I was towards him. I feel raw and in shock and sad – my father doesn't think he has two weeks to live and I think he's right.

Monday, July 24th
• *11:15pm* •

Today was a super excellent day. I was in a great mood, and accomplished so much at work. I also made two decisions. I've decided to do some research at the library, no more than three hours a week on Fridays, for career counselling.

I've been thinking about sex a lot, but am not connected with my feelings. I realize I confuse sex and nurturing. I've had more contact on a sexual level, specifically incest, than on a nurturing level. The bottom line is if I think of sex both as physical and emotional intimacy, then all I want to do is gag. The reality is I still need nurturing, from both women and men, but I need more nurturing from men.

I also found out how my Uncle Caesar responded to my father when he told him about the incest. Mom said that Uncle Caesar just broke down and sobbed, and said the news hurt as much as if it had happened to his own daughter. He said he always liked me, but found it hard to get to know me because I didn't allow anyone close enough. My uncle also removed the picture of Uncle Marco from his bedroom bureau.

I'm really starting to like the way I look and feel and I'm having fewer and fewer ugly days. Yesterday at a meeting two people were sharing their pain with us, how they are trying to deal with incest, but avoid it and run from the pain. They've been in the same place with this issue. Yesterday, I was grateful that my process just blew up in my face because it forced me to face it. I also had the courage and willingness to walk through the nightmare of my childhood again. The pain is slowly fading away. YEAH!!! My uncle the disgusting prick lost the war. Uncle Marco, you're a fuck-up and a dickweed, as Julie would call you. I won, and I have myself and my life back. You lost sucker! I really miss Don a lot. Probably as much as I hate Uncle Marco is as much as I love and respect Don. I can't wait until he comes back from vacation.

Friday, August 4th
● *1:30pm* ●

I'm angry and tired today. I'm at the library and I've spent three hours reading about various career fields. It was kind of boring, but I have to find out what I want to do. I had a great session with Don. I told him how angry I was that he left, and how I felt that I wasn't being heard and if he could suggest that

I was well enough to see him every other week. I told him my sexuality was still nowhere, I still didn't trust guys, nor like them, and my rage and anger were pretty out of control. I told him that I was still sexually shut down and I couldn't even deal with a date. I asked him if he had ever worked with a woman as shut down as myself and did she heal? He said yes, it was definitely possible to heal. He said my sexuality is brand new and the fact that my father is dying just absolutely threw it into a tizzy.

I was talking to Don about affection and touching and explained the realization that I had earlier this week. There are only two people who when they hug me I want to say 'Get off of me!' I feel stifled many of the times. One person is Karen. I always felt she wanted more from me than I was willing or able to give. She is much more demonstrative than I, but her neediness always yelled out. I felt she hugged me for her own need; since her need for affection was so high she held on longer than was necessary. Then, there's Stuart, Antonia's boyfriend; he was involved with an incest survivor and he knows I feel safe with him. Yet what I really want to tell him is that he holds me longer not because of true feelings but to help desensitize me. Don gave an example of working with incest survivors and how they feel in situations like that. He said something about wanting to tear off the face of the person that was crossing the boundaries. That simple statement restored all my trust in him. He actually understands how I feel.

I got some great feedback from Don about Karen. In May, 1987, Karen told me she was gay, which was no surprise to me on a conscious level; on an emotional level it was too threatening at that time. I remained in contact with Karen until December or January of this year. During that time she told me she was in love with me, and I said we could deal with it and just brushed it off emotionally. Then I got to the point that I felt totally stifled and had to let go of her for while. Don said that was when my homophobia exploded and he told me to put the issues with Karen on the shelf because of where I was in the process of recovery.

Don believes that on an unconscious level Karen represented a male to me. She fell in love with me physically, spiritually, and emotionally, but I couldn't even look at it because my own sexuality was so buried. It was only after I had enough space from Karen that I could even begin to look at my own sexuality. During those few months I didn't know if I was gay or not, and Don didn't want the scale to tip toward Karen's way of life if that was not my actual orientation. The sad part is that a lot of mixed messages came from both of us because our sexuality was so screwed up. Don said with reference to my relationship with Karen a lot more will crystalize in time, and it was not helpful to rush any explanations or make amends yet.

Don also said this whole issue with my father dying is affecting my sexuality, but it's also affecting co-dependency issues with my family when the incest came up. At the time I am starting to build a relationship with my family, my father is diagnosed with brain cancer, which throws everyone into a tizzy and I have to remove myself again. He said I'm not able to shut down any longer, so I revert to being an angry, victimized little kid who doesn't trust, and has no hope, and wants to destroy everything around her. He said I was acting out in that way rather than coping with the situation. That explained the anger and violent feelings over the last two weeks. He said my adult and child joined forces and just decided to act out.

I'm very lucky to have a therapist who is a guy and who is funny, sensitive, excellent, and happens to care about me a lot. I saw Lyn last night and it was really good catching up with her.

Thursday, August 10th
● *11:16pm* ●

I had a real angry and funny session with Don tonight. I started to share how I'm not going anywhere, how Lyn came over last night and it's so hard to incorporate the physical, emotional and verbal feelings. I care for her so much and its so hard to show her. Lyn told me to try thinking 'Let go of some' of whatever I'm trying to change. Don said that I have to stop comparing my relationship with Lyn to the one I have with him. They're two very separate relationships. He said I'm still thinking negatively. I'm saying where I'm not, instead of saying I'm glad I can cry with Lyn and hope to become more emotionally spontaneous. He hates my thought process because I always analyze myself and come up with negative conclusions; I drive him crazy with it.

He proceeds to tell me that no one has ever learned how to kiss, be sexual, or have intercourse through a book; you learn through experience. I hate learning through experience. He then suggests I stop hanging out only with my women friends who all have issues of sexual abuse, and start going out on dates. He said I should go to a singles club. I told him 'I'm not going to a fucking club full of rejects.' Then he tells me I should take out a personal ad. I told him an ad in a magazine is about $400; he said he was thinking of papers with a free service. I told him he was fucking stupid; then I stomped my feet, kicked his coffee table and started to cry.

I told him it wasn't fair my stupid father had to die, that I had no girl friends who were out socialising and without boyfriends, that even though I understand his suggestions I wasn't going to listen to any of his fucking ideas. That's when he told me that I should read *Reader's Digest*. I just started laughing, threw his pillows at him, and called him a fucking idiot. Don said that he's read them since he was twelve because the articles are true and hopeful, and at that time he desperately needed that because he was living with active alcoholism in his parents' home.

Now here's the truth: I got so mad at Don because he put a voice to a secret thought. Last week I got mail from my Alumni Association asking me to join their singles group. I said, to myself, 'That might be fun.' Then when Don suggested I do all those stupid things just to meet people, he voiced my need for new friendships, dating, and intimacy. It's one thing to secretly think something; it's another for my therapist to push me towards that.

I'm angry because my father dying brings me face to face with my own mortality, and my need to live my life fully. The bottom line is that I don't have the willingness or energy to go and join clubs or organizations. Next week it may be different; I could respond to ads and not place one. Natalie said that if I keep an open mind I will meet someone. I guess finding out that Kelly got engaged Tuesday didn't help. Someone who never dated, was emotionally and sexually unavailable, and had only one date her whole life, meets this guy at work and less than a year later she's engaged.

Thursday, August 31st
● *10:25pm* ●

Today was a funny and sad day. I left work directly to go to my session with Don and while I was driving I was thinking about dating, and all of a sudden I was in Kennedy Airport instead of the Belt Parkway. Twenty-five minutes later and in bumper to bumper traffic I was back on the road again. Both Don and I got a laugh out of that story.

My session was painful because I found out my paternal grandfather died this morning at 7:00. I called my parents' house to see how things were and my Mom talked to me, and then my Dad asked to talk to me. He broke down sobbing on the phone and all he could say was how he misses his father and he can't even go to his funeral. Don asked me why not. I hadn't kept Don up to date on my Dad's health but now he weighs only 145 pounds and he's a tall guy. He sways when he walks and he passed out in the bathroom. He has just been accepted into a hospice program once the radiation treatments are over. The criterion for a hospice is six months or less left to live. I told Don that my grandfather died and that I'm shut down. When Don understood how much my father's cancer had progressed, he said, 'Of course you're shut down. To face your grandfather's death you would have to face your own father's death.'

I started to cry and when I looked up, Don's face was all red and he was crying too. I ignored that fact. I can't deal with the fact that Don cares, loves, and sympathizes so much that he can cry at my pain and maybe some of his own. I'll acknowledge it next week, but I couldn't right then and there.

I told Don that now five out of nine of my Dad's brothers and sisters, including my father, know my story. Today I realized that three months ago I hadn't even known if I was going tell my own father and now they know. I told my father he could tell whoever he wanted, except his four remaining brothers and sisters because either they don't respect boundaries or I have no relationship with them. My Dad and Mom told my aunt and uncles; two are like parent figures and two have small children under eleven. The uncle who was told last asked if the perpetrator was my grandfather. Very interesting at the least.

Also, last night I spoke with my father and he said how much he hates undressing when he goes to the doctor; he'd rather die. My father is very private and prudish about walking in his boxers. Last night I asked my Dad if, before his father passed away, he thought his father had ever molested anyone in his family. He said no because his father was physically private too. I don't buy that as a reason. I still believe my grandfather incested someone, if only Uncle Marco.

Sunday, September 3rd
● *11:45pm* ●

The backlash from Friday's awareness has been severe and I've used everything not to feel, but it didn't work. It started to come up last night, the feeling of being out of control; I ate cookies, danced for two hours and was still hyper. So afterward I stopped and bought the *New York Times*, a package of Yodels, and a candy bar. After I dropped Natalie off, I bought a pack of cigarettes. At home I smoked and crawled into bed, and all I could do was shake. I finally realized that my splitting had integrated, and I had no control over my father dying; somehow I got the feeling of being out of control just like when the incest was occurring. I left my body and was spinning out into space and all I felt was terror.

When I woke up this morning I had ten minutes to get ready and be at my parent's house, and I smoked some more there. I also cried with my father; he couldn't even take off his shirt to take a nap. I had to do it for him. My mother said she wanted to call me yesterday because she was worried about me. She said that when I finally realized how I had been coping with Daddy dying my eyes almost popped out of my head.

I realized then why I was having all this backlash. My attitude was that I fucked it up for today so why not end the day with a cigarette? Tonight while I was getting ready to go to bed I got on my knees and asked not to smoke. I've finally realized that yes, I'm out of control, yes, I am powerless over the fact that my father is dying. I resorted to all old destructive coping mechanisms in order not to feel out of control.

I don't want to smoke or eat sugar or hurt myself in any other way, but that feeling of being out of control and zooming into space was so terrifying. It's taken almost twenty-four hours to come down to earth. Ten minutes ago is when I finally realized that I'm powerless and out of control about my father's situation. I don't know how to live with that feeling of being out of my body lost in space and out of control. I didn't even tell Lyn because I didn't know what was going on until 5:00 tonight when I spoke with my Mom. She said she's not surprised that I had backlash.

Thursday, September 14th
● *10:49pm* ●

I'm feeling so much better. I went to therapy and I'll be going to work on Friday. Don and I discussed my Dad and the issue of control. Don reminded me that the only reason I'm going to see my father is for my benefit, not to be a source of support for my family. I feel a lot better just not seeing him this week. We also spoke about control. Don said my thoughts are controlling, my assumptions are controlling and the simple fact that I think I'm going to feel terror if I let go of control is controlling. He said that controlling feeds onto itself with a second by-product: a crisis. He said this past year has been full of crises that were self-created. He said my child knows only crises that have to do with fear, despair, and hopelessness. I told him that recovery in itself brings about crises through change, but they are of hope, excitement, and fun – something my little girl knows very little of. Each time I predict an outcome or make a formula for a plan including the results, I'm controlling. Don calls me 'the controller.'

He said I'm like Spock in *Star Trek* who was totally logical, but it was the humans with feelings who came up with the solutions.

Don said I should try to feel my feelings whether I'm at work or wherever. He said I might feel some release. I don't know why, but I feel somewhat hopeful and excited. Maybe there is some hope in all this. I do know and feel that my controlling is hurting me, and it's limiting my choices. Don reminded me about a Higher Power; it could be him, Lyn, a meeting, etc., but I need to have one.

Sunday, September 17th

● *9:18pm* ●

Yesterday, I spoke with Lyn about comforting, nurturing, and love. It was a beautiful intimate conversation. That woman really loves me a great deal. I got in touch with the fact that by detaching from my family I'm facing the issue of loss; I have distanced from my family and I can feel the feelings. I also realized that I've lost my mother again. With my father dying she's really focused on my father and is also playing the martyr because she's not letting others do things for my father; but she's also losing herself. It's sad because I started to have a relationship with her and she's gone away again.

There's an ache inside that I'm finally beginning to hear and it's an empty feeling. Lyn says it's the feeling of being all alone and by myself with my pain. We talked about my fears of being comforted – that I'll just dissolve and be a puddle on the floor, or, she said, that I won't be able to let go because the need is so great.

Sunday, September 24th

● *10:40pm* ●

I have some catching up to do. On Thursday, I started to talk to Don about my struggle of letting Lyn nurture and comfort me and how she definitely represents my mother in this area. We started to talk about touching and nurturing with my immediate family and I shared some awareness that I had from doing the exercise on touching from the workbook *Repeat After Me* by Claudia Black, but how I didn't want to talk to Lyn or Don about it yet. All of a sudden, I couldn't breathe in Don's office; talking about my family, and about touching and feeling good, and about the make-up class, and about looking at guys and their looking back, was a lot to admit all at once. When Don told me I was beginning to realize that I was pretty, attracted to guys, and that I looked pretty in session I could no longer breathe. I told him I wanted to slither beneath the door and go home.

Don asked if it was because I felt slimy, and I said yes. Don said my sexuality is starting to emerge, but I deny all my feelings whatsoever when I look at guys. Out of nowhere, I told Don there's a little box on the right side of my brain and in it there's shame. When I saw Lyn later on I came to realize I'm still repulsed by my kid, and I'm afraid that Lyn will be totally repulsed by my kid if she were to hold her. Then Lyn asked me a hard question; she asked if there was any part of the incest that I could have enjoyed? It's strange that she asked me the question because this thought has been popping up in my head for the last week and it won't go away.

One of the things about guys I was always attracted to was their legs. This goes pretty far back. I could block a guy's whole body out, but still look at his legs. I wondered if this has any connection with remembering legs rubbing against my genitals as a kid. I don't know when this happened, at what stage of the incest; I believe it was my uncle but I'm not even sure. I also told Lyn how hard it is for me to tell her the compliment I received from Don. She said my uncle may have given me very strong verbal messages to make me react that way.

She said that I can get the love, support, and nurturing from her and she doesn't have to represent my mother, but a friend. My mother has abandoned me twice, but Lyn said she won't. She also said that it's not my kid's fault that my family is not available for her today. She did nothing wrong. Lyn thinks that somehow my kid is blaming herself. She also said that if I don't let Lyn nurture me, I'll continue to be self-abusive such as eating sugar and believing that since my family isn't available again, then no one is available, that I am all alone.

Lyn helped me realize that shame is coming up because it's been intertwined with nurturing my whole life when it shouldn't have been. Now that I'm letting Lyn hold me, the feeling of shame needs to be looked at and separated away from love, nurturing, and comfort.

Saturday, September 30th
● *10:52pm* ●

About touching: I've no memory of my mother's touch as a child. I know she was always present, but there's a big void there partly because of my being an incest survivor and partly because of her own sexual abuse issues. My mother has kissed and hugged me on birthdays, holidays, and for academic achievements, but everyday nurturing, hugs, and kisses didn't exist. However, my father was very affectionate. If we didn't say good morning and kiss him and my mother, he would send us back to our rooms and make us start the day again. I always tolerated being kissed and hugged by my father. I thought it was a fake gesture because he was emotionally unavailable. I do remember getting into wrestling matches with my father, but unfortunately I would always get hurt or cry because I was too stubborn to give in and lose. My father didn't know when to stop.

My brother is very affectionate and demonstrative. I got a lot of nurturing through spending time with him as a toddler and small child. My brother was safe to kiss, hug, and hold. Even as he got older and was able to get me into a headlock, he was safe. The only time my brother wasn't safe was for the first year and a half I was dealing with incest; my brother was the same age as Uncle Marco and he was male. The only time I've been repulsed by my brother was when he was trying to manipulate me and had me pinned against the dining room wall and was kissing me to try to get his way. I just shut down and told him if he didn't get off of me I would throw him across the room. I had a body pinning me down and I was trapped.

With Annamarie the only memories of touch I have with her are either fighting or being tickled and kissed. She is very mushy and affectionate, and I hated it.

Vanessa was the lost child growing up and I simply hated her. I didn't go anywhere near her because she grated my soul, but I didn't know why. Today I know I saw my own lost child and victimization in Vanessa.

Jessica has been a very big part of my healing in the area of touch. Jessica is a warm, affectionate, loving, cute, bright, seven-year-old child. She somehow mirrored my own child. I always kiss her hello and goodbye, tell her how pretty she is, and comb her hair. Jessica and I have even cried together over my Dad dying.

With my extended family I only kissed them hello and good-bye out of obligation; when they were at my house I usually stayed away. If I had my own way, I wouldn't even have seen almost all of them while growing up.

As a child the word 'touch' meant crossing boundaries, pain, terror, malicious intentions, being out of control, feeling dirty, legs rubbing against my genital area, being tickled, wanting something from me, comforting someone else, being insincere, being manipulative, not being in my own body, losing all sense of progression, not being able to stop the touching, and being repulsed. Touching was always for someone else's benefit.

After reading what touching meant to me, Lyn went over each item of what touch meant to me in reference to my uncle, and I explained what my child's fears were. What I came to realize is that my child believes that if you love someone too much (which means he or she intimately knows my kid as well as my adult), then he or she either goes away or betrays her. I started to feel very sad. Lyn said my child only has a frame of reference of sexual touch and not of nurturing, comforting touch. My child believes that nurturing touch automatically leads to sexual touch. In addition, she's afraid that she won't be heard if for some reason she needs the touching to stop and therefore will be victimized.

I started to cry and like a little kid asked Lyn if I could get my teddy bear. As I was holding my bear, I started to shut down so I gave my bear to Lyn and told her that my little girl sits with her knees under her chin all alone and cries. I wanted to sit that way, but I let Lyn hold me. I sat for five minutes six inches away from Lyn and was unable to ask her to hold me. She said the only way I'll be able to separate nurturing and sex is by taking the risk and finding out. I did ask Lyn to hold me and I broke down sobbing in her arms until I was cried out.

I've been waiting and wanting to do that for a very long time. I'm completely exhausted, but really proud of my little kid. As I was sobbing, I called my uncle a stupid dick and cried that he was wrong, my kid isn't slimy at all. It was my uncle who was slimy. He was the disgusting one. Lyn said as I continue to be nurtured and comforted I will be able to work through the slime.

October 8th

• *5:04pm* •

It's strange, but I seem to be getting what I need. Yesterday, I had lunch with Natalie and we chatted. She was able to share her struggles and joys of being in an intimate, healthy relationship. She's having a hard time having an orgasm with her boyfriend. She has never been able to do that, and she knows it's related to control and incest. Her boyfriend said that they need to take time out during sex if she's not feeling anything, that he is in no rush. She said she never imagined an intimate relationship like this.

She always thought love was sex and now really knows differently. He was the one who brought up the topic of sex and her achieving an orgasm; now they are able to talk about this very intimate stuff. I knew I was getting what I needed because the message I was getting was that there are guys out there who are willing to wait and work with me on issues of sex, if he cares about me and the relationship. I also felt sad because I don't think I'm anywhere near that yet, but I'm getting better. Just the fact that I could even listen to this intimate sexual discussion is an improvement. When we were all in Jamaica and they were talking about blow jobs, I got up and told them I had go, and went jogging along the shore to deal with the anxiety.

Friday, October 27th

• *10:10pm* •

It's been a brutal week. Every day seems like a month. It appeared at first that my Dad had had a stroke. My Dad is totally paralyzed on the left side and he can no longer walk. I visited him tonight. When we tried to get him to bed his boxer shorts fell round his ankles and he bent down so that I wouldn't see him exposed. My aunt got him together and was able to help him to bed. I left so he wouldn't feel humiliated, and I went to the backyard and sobbed my eyes out. The doctor called back and explained that the tumor had swelled and it was pressing on a nerve that affects his motor control. The next stage is that my father will begin to have mental confusion. I talked to my mother tonight about getting him to a hospice and she said she can't do that yet.

My Daddy is now going to leave forever. This is so painful that I couldn't stop shaking. I bought a pack of cigarettes and then left them at my parents' after smoking six of them. I called Lyn from my parents' house and told her what had just happened and cried. She said she'll call me back just to check on me later tonight. This is becoming agonizing. I called Don, too, and cried with him. I can't believe this is happening. My Dad had told me that I looked great tonight. I was wearing my red suit.

On a positive note I swam three times this week and by the third day I was having backlash. I got a flashback of my uncle trying to drown me. He had his hand on the back of my head and my arms and legs were kicking and my arms were moving wildly because I couldn't breathe. I started to have an anxiety attack, so I called Lyn from work to overcome the fear and went swimming afterwards. I don't want that disgusting prick to win, so I'm going to keep on swimming and take lessons. I even survived having the people I work with see me in a bathing suit.

November 5th

• *8:30am* •

I've been at the hospital since 8:00 am. It's quiet and safe, just myself and my father. So much has happened since Monday.

My father went into a semi-coma where he lost consciousness and his ears turned blue; we almost lost him. The medicine he took for seizures and pressure in his brain were not being ingested in his blood when he took them orally. They gave it to him intra-venously and by Tuesday night my whole family was laughing and joking with him. He said he almost kicked the bucket.

On Wednesday, my father had some mental confusion and continued to talk non-stop. I played basketball because the pool was closed and I beat the crap out of the ball. By Thursday I was enraged and wanted to kill my boss and then selected members of my extended family. I saw Don and was able to dump all the rage. It just isn't fair. Why wasn't my maniac aunt who is of no use to anyone, or my uncle, or his son, chosen to die since both could win the 'Dick of the Year' award. I was finally able to cry in Don's office. I had been emotionally shut down so far. I had started to smoke.

On Thursday I was around safe people at work, Don and Lyn, and I was able to feel. Don suggested very strongly that I speak with my father and say some sort of goodbye. I decided to do it on Friday. I went to visit Lyn and it was good to feel safe again.

On Friday, when I saw my Dad, he was totally senile. Within forty-eight hours my father had gone from being coherent to being a little boy. I told him everything I was going to miss about him, and he kept changing the subject and reminiscing. Yesterday and today he's been complaining more and more of headaches and being in pain. So I finally told the doctor I want pain-killers on demand because we were promised my father would not be in pain.

A big realization occurred yesterday. I've been struggling not to smoke since last week and I realized that I don't feel safe around any of my family, especially my extended family. I realized smoking was one way to protect myself from them so I thought smoking would shut down the feelings and keep me safe. Then I went to a meeting and the topic was on detachment and I realized I haven't detached from my extended family. I need to seperate and protect myself from their denial and insanity. I also feel like shit and it might be the beginning of bronchitis and I don't want to be sick. So I threw out the pack of cigarettes last night at 10:00 pm; it's almost 11:00 am and I haven't picked up a cigarette.

For the past two days I've been here at the hospital at 8:00 am and it's only been my father and myself. I've been able to cry while he slept. I'm very angry that my father is dying, and what I want to do is beat the fucking shit out of my maniac aunt. She's so critical I really wish she'd just fuck off and die instead of my father. But that's not reality. I think I'm doing OK considering what's going on.

My friends have been great, calling me, reaching out, and just letting me know they're there.

• *10:00pm* •

It's exactly twenty-four hours since I had a cigarette and I've cried twice. My other aunt came to visit my father today, and she cried while he slept most of the day. I got so angry and I didn't even know that I was or why I felt so angry. I literally had the back of my chair to her and read the paper while she cried. I shut down totally.

When I spoke to Lyn and told her what was going on she gave me some really good feedback. My extended family is able to mourn. Lyn reminded me of the fact that I feel betrayed by these people and I shut down because their mourning and sobbing brings me back to twenty-three years ago when everyone was mourning my uncle's death and I felt invisible. I don't want their grief and hurt to touch me. I wasn't to able to say fuck off and walk away.

I try to accept others' feelings and their right to mourn and have these special times with my father too. This is getting very painful. First my father wasn't emotionally available for me, and now he won't be physically present either. I was able to sob in Lyn's arms and when she held me really close, I felt secure not trapped.

Wednesday, November 15th

● *7:50pm* ●

I've crashed. I didn't go to work today because I'm fighting something. I've had the shakes and chills since Sunday and I just slept all day. I'm finally paying the price for smoking. I hope I have the willingness to stop. Today my father was moved to a new facility within the hospital for acute care patients. I feel like absolute shit – physically and emotionally. Everything just hurts. I realize that I've been playing this tape in my head that said I'm not allowed to cry at work or anywhere else because my father hasn't died and no one will believe me. Since then I've been trying not to hold my feelings back. I feel so weak, like I'm going to dissolve. On Monday when I spoke with Lyn, I was very angry at God.

I hate the God I grew up with and I am tired of that notion of believing 'you're never given more than you can handle.' I asked Lyn if Lisa Steinberg, the little girl that died two years ago, was given only what she could handle. There must be some sense to this because I loathe and despise the Catholic Church and the Catholic God I grew up with, but there is a spiritual need I have which I'm not fully in touch with.

I've decided to start feeling, writing, and talking about the God I grew up with because I feel totally defeated and all this rage is within me. The reality is that I can't feel worse than I do right now. I went to Catholic school for only three months in first grade and then I went to Italy with my father. The only memory I have is the nun having a big wooden fish with a rhinestone eye, which she would hold by the tail as a handle and punish the kids by hitting them in the rear. I went to public school my whole life except for college and I chose to go there. Throughout religious education in elementary and junior high school I learned of a loving God and went to mass on Sunday.

In high school I was involved with the folk group, parish council, two retreat programs as a participant and then I was a group leader, as well as working at the parish day camp for four summers where I started out as a counselor and became assistant director. All my extra-curricular activities were church-related and

I somehow met all my friends through the church. In college I was part of campus ministry, the hunger walk coordinator, member of the outreach team to high school students, and still worked retreats for high school kids. My first therapist was a priest who was a friend of my family and who I went to speak to at the end of my junior year in college. I was in a community that was totally safe because they were emotionally unavailable, where 'doing' was a big plus and where God loved you.

I was able to hide because I was the doer, too busy doing to feel my feelings or face my sexuality. That system is so fucked up. Why didn't anyone say there's something wrong with it? Why wasn't anyone aware of the fact that I was asexual, emotionally dead and just running as fast as I could? I was surrounded by people who had worked with teenagers for years and yet couldn't see how fucked up I was. I even went to a priest therapist who never even brought up the issue of sex, or the fact that I didn't even talk about it at twenty-one years old.

When I was going to meetings to work through issues about my alcoholic family, I stopped going to church, but was able to go back when the acceptance came and the rage left. Then the incest came up and I was going to church and hanging on for dear life because of the terror I was feeling. I believed in Catholicism even when I first realized I was an incest survivor. But four months later, when I remembered the physical abuse and almost dying because of it, I realized that I'd believed in the fairy tale of the Catholic Church in order to keep the reality of my childhood buried. How could there be a loving God after what happened to me? The fucking Catholic Church prized virginity so highly, and I lost the prize at the age of five-and-a-half, and it wasn't even my fault. I lost twenty-two years of a very strong belief system and was left with a gaping hole.

When I realized that not only was I an incest survivor, but also a physically abused child, all my trust, hope and faith, were gone except for Lyn and Don. Through surviving the pain and starting to get a second chance, I've started gaining a spiritual sense, but I never let go of the rage, betrayal, and resentment of the God I grew up with.

I've got off the telephone with Lyn and it was very helpful.

Lyn said that I need to take suggestions and become humble once again. She said the definition for humility is to become teachable. When I started smoking two weeks ago I tried to do it my old distractive way, and I failed. Lyn also helped me realize that I've accepted my father's death; I'm the only one being open about the severity of his health. I'm the only one who says 'semi-coma'; everyone else says he's 'sleeping'. Lyn said that I'm battling their denial constantly, and I'm punishing myself for accepting my feelings. I can lose myself when I'm constantly battling other people's denial. So, the hard time I'm having is with my family and their alcoholic denial system.

My father never reached sobriety, never got to know me fully, and we never had intimacy in our relationship.

God

God, I still agree that you are a greedy fucking pig. I don't trust you or your process; I believe the Catholic Church is a total sham of individuals who hide behind you in order to not deal with reality. You are just a fucking band-aid and not a source of healing. I haven't healed because of my faith in you, going to church, even praying. I've been healing because of my desire to live, my defiance and my intense hatred of you, the church and my uncle.

It's time to stop wasting so much energy in hating you; I'm letting go and getting rid of you from my life. In many ways I was betrayed by you just like my uncle. I was taught that you were a loving God. If you were so loving, how do you explain the abuse of a five-and-a-half-year-old? How do you explain the blood, and the terror? Yes, my uncle was the perpetrator but you're God. I'm supposed to turn my life and will to your care. If you decide who lives or dies, you could have either killed my uncle sooner or protected me. I hate your fucking guts, I wasted so much time, energy, love and faith for something that was total bullshit. I can't even begin to express the loathing I have towards you, your fucking church, and all it represents. It's all a farce, which I believed in so desperately.

There's a big spiritual void in my life; I miss a sense of community, a sense of family, and a sense of peace, but I would rather miss all this than believe in God or the Catholic Church. I've lost a great deal in my life so I'll survive this loss too. I just want to stop wasting my energy and rage on someone and some system I loathe. God, you've made another mistake once again. It's nothing new in my life, but you picked the wrong person to die. I could name at least three who deserve it more. There's no rhyme nor reason or sense, but there never is with you. You're a total fuck up and I will never believe in you or your fucked up Church. Have I said just how much I hate you? You are a Fucking Greedy Pig!

Sunday, December 2nd

I love starting new journals. I always feel like I get a second chance or that there is still hope. This new journal I got for my birthday. Even though it's tomorrow, we started celebrating last night at Gena's. Today was a really good day. So far, birthday loot is tickets to *Erasure* and a pound of imported decaf coffee. We all went to Gena's for coffee and cake and we just laughed all night. Antonia, Gena, and I arrived first and we got to talking about orgasms, and I'm going to buy this book called *For Yourself*. I think it's time because I'm feeling really horny and there's no release because I'm not even able to achieve an orgasm by myself.

I saw Don tonight and it was actually a lot of fun. I admitted to him that I wanted to start dating and have a boyfriend. He literally tipped his chair backwards and rolled out of his chair. He said such an admission deserved such a reaction, that I was getting healthy. All I could do was laugh and call him a fool. I can't believe to what lengths he goes to make a point! This is celebration. It felt really nice.

I shared with him about seeing Karen, and needing to speak to her but not knowing what really happened. I realized that I felt so betrayed by Karen waiting three years before telling me she was gay, and because my incest issues were emerging. I realized that I didn't respond when her mother died because her neediness frightened me and made me feel like I had a noose around my neck. Her neediness had stifled me in the past. I felt that I was the only emotionally available person she had in her life. When she told me she was in love with me, I totally shut down. Karen was affectionate and demonstrative, but I was not able to tell the difference; I thought any touch was sexual and felt unsafe. In addition, I cut myself off from my own sexuality, and I did not know if I was gay or not and I was terrified to find out I might be. So, when Karen told me she was in love with me I closed up and pulled away. When I spoke to Don, I told him that I do care about her deeply. He said we had a very intimate relationship and maybe it's time for me to make amends.

Tuesday, December 5th

• *10:25pm* •

I had a wonderful birthday weekend. On Saturday, I went out to dinner with Natalie and Rick. We never got to see *Steel Magnolias* because the tickets were sold out and then Sunday we had another birthday celebration with Antonia, Erica and Natalie; then I had dinner with my family and I got some pretty nice cards and gifts. I have had a special birthday.

Last night at the hospital with my Dad I called my mother; she told me that she had called the cops because my brother was verbally and physically abusive and intimidating. He had threatened Vanessa and destroyed part of her room. Once the cops got there, he told them not to worry because he was packing and would be leaving. He came back later to pick up a check that he was getting from his insurance but which he really was supposed to give my mother since he owed her money. However, legally the check was his. In essence, then, he stole from my mother. The cops advised my mother to change the locks, which she did. I'm really proud of her for standing up to my brother. I really believe that my brother is on drugs. This is the second time he has come home at 11:00 after being out with his friends, and started a fight and ended up becoming enraged and physically abusive in some way.

I talked about all this in group last night and everyone told me to worry about myself, and if my mother or family should bring up the behavior of my brother I could tell them that I can't deal with it. I've decided to physically detach myself, and I mean it. I'm not going over, and I'm not phoning. By becoming part of my family's problems, I take the focus off myself, my recovery, my goals, and I become physically ill.

On top of all this, my mother calls me; she tells me that she was upset that I brought up the fact that my father is an alcoholic in front of Jessica in family therapy. I just lost it. I got angry with her and told her that I was tired of her denial and she made the choice to go to a recovery program for Jessica and herself for families of alcoholics; for she doesn't have to be the martyr and do it all herself. I asked her if she was going to deal with Dad's alcoholism after his death, or if she would put him on a pedestal and put the alcoholism under the rug. She said she can't deal with Jessica's questions at the moment and the real issue is that Dad is dying.

I said no. The real issue is that we're a dysfunctional alcoholic family without coping skills and the shit is finally hitting the fan because my Dad is dying. I said it's like there's an elephant in the living room which no one is noticing. Suddenly the elephant takes a crap, and everyone says the shit is the problem. My Dad dying of brain cancer is not why my family acts insane; the fact that we have a family disease called alcoholism is the reason. The fact that my father is an alcoholic is the issue.

I told my mother that I will take Jessica to a recovery program for children in alcoholic families when I go to my own meeting, but the real problem is not Jessica's questions, but my mother's denial. My mother told me that I was too direct and she was gentler. I told her that was bullshit. I told my mother that she was as direct as I, except when she wants to stay in denial. I also told her that she may want to play the martyr and totally wrap herself up in my father's illness, but not to put these expectations on me. If that's what she wanted, she could knock herself out, but she was forfeiting the six other people in my family, including herself, for a man who is lucid for only a small part of the time and who could continue to be in that condition for a year or more. I said that for a seven-year-old child, meaning Jessica, a year was an eternity and my mother would be repeating the past once again – like I was ignored by her when I was in

Italy at five and a half years old, my mother is ignoring Jessica's needs, this time because my father is sick.

This last part brought up a lot of pain, and another core issue for me. I have very little compassion for the lost-child role, the one that is hurt, and I realized why on Saturday. An incident happened in the hospital on Saturday that made me realize everyone but me had ignored Jessica and the fact that she was in a hospital at her age. I suddenly realized the past was being repeated, that my mother had tunnel vision only for my father and we children were being ignored once again. Lyn helped me realize that my child was ignored as well. I realized that there's a lot of anger, lack of respect, and hurt mostly towards my mother because she ignored me; because I was a 'good girl', I had been easy to ignore. When I see needy people, or the lost child in adults, who are hurting I always get angry. Anger covers the realization that I was ignored my whole life by my family; they never saw that I was different. In turn I continued to ignore myself. Today, the more I let nurturing and comfort into my life, the more I get in touch with the child who was ignored and became the lost child.

I'm sobbing my eyes out because I have realized that I was ignored by my family as a child and adolescent; I was also ignored by friends, and most especially by guys. The agony of being a teenager is back. It's a miracle that I'm alive today. I was so emotionally suicidal in high school and college and I didn't even know it. If nothing else was achieved by this conversation with my mother, I was able to see my mother's denial, my family's insanity and a lifetime of being ignored. I've decided that I've been ignoring myself too long and I am not willing to live my life that way any longer.

Sunday, December 17th

• *4:25pm* •

My father died yesterday morning. We're getting ready for the wake that is tonight and tomorrow. The funeral is Tuesday morning. I put together three photo collages for the wake of my Dad. I just heard *Silent Night* on the radio and started to cry; it was my Dad's favorite song. I can't believe he's gone, forever. It's so final. We all went out to breakfast this morning; it was really nice. Since yesterday we've cried and laughed a lot. I'm scared to go to the wake. This is so fucking hard and unfair. I never had a father and now he's gone.

● *11:55pm* ●

I'm back home. The wake was really hard. My Dad looked really ugly in the coffin, but he was wearing his favorite clothes. Many of my Dad's friends from Italy were there as well as most of my family. My closest friends were there and some people who I haven't seen since running retreats in high school and college; Roxanne and her family, as well as Frank who I haven't seen for five years.

I was really close to Frank while we were working retreats and then we just lost contact. He said he always asked about me through Roxanne, and asked her to tell me that he was thinking about me. He said when you love someone unconditionally, you accept where they are and he knew I needed my space. He said it was in God's time that we'd meet this way at the wake. When I saw him, I just broke down crying in the hallway of the funeral parlor and it was then that I realized how much I missed him.

Antonia, Stuart, and Frank and myself went to dinner after the wake and I told Frank that I'd get in touch with him real soon. I promised him that we would exchange numbers, have him over for dinner, and talk all night like we did when I was in college. I'm really glad I saw him tonight.

Everyone loved the photo collages, and I'm glad I put them together. Lyn, Alice, Karen, and Jennifer came. I got to sit with Lyn for a bit and hold her hand. I was thinking – it's at times like these that I would love to have a boyfriend, just so I could be held and feel alive in someone's arms. I don't know when, or how or who, but I do believe it will happen to me someday.

1990

1996

Sunday, July 15th
● *10:40pm* ●

Yesterday when I spoke to Lyn she said that I should have tried to go out dancing with someone else instead of canceling my plans. I told her there was no one to go out dancing with. She said I should try to talk to guys at meetings who aren't married. I went to a meeting that I haven't been to in some months. I ran into a young guy, Brian, whom I met two years ago. When I ran into him last year he asked me to go out for coffee afterwards, but I had made plans with Natalie, and anyway I was too scared because I saw there was a mutual attraction. I told him I wasn't free, but that I would take a rain check. It was so strange because at first I didn't notice him at the meeting until I moved to the front, sat on the floor and turned round; and there he was. He said hi and kissed me hello. I was glad to see him. I couldn't remember his name, but he had remembered mine. We talked and just kidded around. This guy has sexy legs that I could just get lost in. I realized that my attraction was stronger this time. The recovery process has helped me heal a great deal.

I'm writing because I'm feeling a little scared because I was fantasizing about Brian last night and this morning and I woke up with my vagina actually hurting and sore and I knew I was having bodily recall from incest. I just felt sad and still do. I'm trying not to feel sad or project into the future about Brian. He was talking to his friend and I said goodbye across the room and he blew me a kiss. Walking to my car, I wanted to go back and ask him if he wanted to go out for ice-cream after the meeting, but I got scared. So instead I got into my car and started to drive away when I saw Brian leaving the meeting. I called out to him and asked him if he wanted to go for ice-cream. He said he wasn't free, he was going out with his friend. He said last time I wasn't free and this time he's not. He asked me for my phone number. I hope he calls.

Monday, July 16th

● *10:20pm* ●

I spoke with my Mom and Lyn. I went to my Mom's after eating breakfast in the park because I was just feeling hurt. I was feeling the feelings of being all alone and I didn't want it to be that way. But when I went over to the house it was really hectic, so I made plans for my mother to come over; all I wanted her to do was hold me.

I used this sick day very well. I completed my mortgage application for my co-op, and I took a bubble bath. I was really hurting inside, but it wouldn't come out. My Mom was talking to my aunt earlier in the week about my incest, and my aunt said, 'Where was everyone while I was in Italy, why didn't they see?' My Mom said my grandfather ate breakfast and went to the piazza for the day, my father was having a nervous breakdown due to manic depression, and my grandmother was cooking him seventeen meals a day so he would get better. That's how my grandmother handled everything. My youngest aunt was dating her present husband, and my maniac aunt put her daughter into boarding school so she could socialize and show off with the townspeople, so Uncle Marco was my baby sitter – and my Mom was home in the states.

When my mother said this, my stomach turned. The feeling of being trapped was so powerful. I felt so hurt because I'd really loved Uncle Marco. I idolized him and he shattered all that was pure and innocent about being a child. I was finally able to cry a little with my mother. I'm feeling hurt and depressed but taking today off was a really good idea. I needed to regroup. I also realized that I've been doing too much. I'm home during the week, but I bury my feelings until the weekend comes. Then I'm having, or trying to have, fun; so, when do I get to feel my feelings? I'm going to try to let them happen. Lyn said to try to focus on the positive.

So I'll ask my Higher Power to remove these feelings of shame and fear so I can grow. I also told Lyn that I was eating ice-cream Friday, a bagel yesterday, and today I'm just being defiant. She said it might be because my father was no help while he was in Italy and I'm turning that anger inward instead of on him.

Tuesday, July 17th
• *9:17pm* •

I did something I haven't done in a long time. I took my broom, placed the pillows on the right side of the bed and beat the shit out of the pillows and started to cry. I've been depressed, and today and yesterday I felt waterlogged because I couldn't cry. I don't know who that body was, whether it was my father or uncle while they were in Italy. I'm just furious that I believe being a woman is a liability, that I'm terrified of my sexuality and that every part of my sexuality was shattered because of incest. The two men I loved the most were total fuck-ups, and the men I have been in love with are unavailable. I decided to let someone other than myself pay the price of my defiance, so I beat the pillows.

Why should I hurt myself with all this rage when it belongs to my father and uncle? I realized that by facing and talking about my sexuality with Don all the fear and shame comes up because it's not mutual, and that kicks up the feelings of shame and fear while the incest was going on. When I went to my father for protection, he wasn't available either so the shame and fear belong totally to me.

Today, I'm paying the price for my uncle's rapes and violations and my father's absence. I'm furious not only that my father didn't believe me, but that he was totally uncaring. Today, I miss a warm body because I was truly honest and yet my father was never there for me until the last six months of his life when he was dying.

I keep coming up with unavailable men whether it be emotionally, physically, paternally, sexually, or for protection. I have yet to meet a guy that is both emotionally and physically safe; and yet I'm terrified of my own feelings, sexuality, and of being a woman today.

Wednesday, July 18th

• *9:35pm* •

I woke up this morning and I was extremely nauseous. All the way to work I hoped I wouldn't get sick, but I was gagging. I had to leave work at 2:30. I went to *Woolworths* and bought a plastic baseball bat. I went home and beat the crap out of my uncle (who was the pillow on my bed); I realize I was so nauseous because I had had the sensation of having my uncle's penis in my throat. As I was beating the pillow, I was screaming inside 'Get out of my throat. Get your penis out of there. Get out!!' I was totally exhausted and I slept for two hours afterwards.

When I told Lyn, she said that was great. I told her that I'm tired of having the incest affect my life. She said I'm exhausted because I'm in a battle and I'm fighting for my sexuality. She said I was angry at my Dad because he was supposed to protect me, and he didn't, and the betrayal is felt again as I struggle. Lyn said she's seen me depressed and angry these past few weeks and I couldn't get in touch with these feelings until they surfaced.

I talked to her about my job and I got some clarity. I realized that I still don't know what I want to do or what field I want to work in. Lyn said I'm making myself frazzled by trying to force a job change. I told her the fact that I'm in the same job means I haven't grown and that I'm still dealing with incest. I reached the bottom of my recovery process while I was working there, and I feel that the incest won't have any power in my life when I leave. The fact that I'm still there makes me feel the incest is still affecting me. Lyn said I'm trying to mend myself through my job. The reality is I am still in the process of recovery and I have grown in that period. I told her I'm still viewed as a kid at work; by changing jobs I'll be viewed as an adult. Lyn said maturity comes from within, not from a job. She said the reality is that if I took another job I might not have a job because of my past absences. She suggested I apply to school; she really believes I'll get some direction from school and I'll also meet someone and date. I should stop complaining about my job and focus on dealing with my sexuality, buying the co-op, and starting school.

Those are more than enough changes. She said I will feel

less frazzled the more I listen to my Higher Power because I'll get what I need in reference to answers. She said she doesn't believe I'm meant to be there forever, but it's where I'm meant to be at the moment.

I'm going to try to accept where I am right now. This is so hard, but part of me really knows I need to deal with my sexuality and get into a relationship before I change jobs, because I can get lost in work so easily.

I pretended I was beating my uncle's face in while beating the pillows with the bat. I'm determined to let my sexuality out and kill my uncle's abusive presence. I realize the scar will always be there, but the wound is still healing so I don't have the scar yet.

July 20th
● *7:01pm* ●

I got my answer as to why I have been obsessed with changing jobs. It came from *Healing the Shame that Binds You*: 'Toxic shame is about being; no amount of doing will ever change it' (Bradshaw 64). I had an awareness tonight after reading several pages from the book. Anything I was ever embarrassed about became my shame because my eyes only perceived through the perspective of shame. As a result of the incest and physical abuse, everything became my shame. I felt shame over my father's manic depression, his accent, my family because the incest was from a member of this 'perfect Italian family'. I felt shame about the clothes I wore, how my body looked, how I looked as a little girl in third or fourth grade. I have no memory of first or second grade. This shame is not about incest but about me. I've taken my uncle's shame and interwoven it into my soul and made it my own.

My shame went from not being able to cry to having flashbacks and recall, to smells that occurred during the abuse. I feel like a walking stop watch that has recorded everything negative during twenty-three years but which has very little frame of reference pertaining to positive things. I don't want to lose anything more to shame. I don't know that I can regain myself from the shame. I don't remember what it's like to believe that I'm not shamed. This is so painful.

Wednesday, July 25th
• *10:56pm* •

I spoke to Lyn tonight and I told her about how I asked my mother to hold me last night and then proceeded to eat sugar and smoke two cigarettes because the fear was back. I told her I don't want to heal this way. I asked her if it would be better if I put Bradshaw's book down and started to read *Incest and Sexuality*. She said she thought that was a great idea. I don't want to abuse myself through this process. Lyn said my defiance is still powerful. I swam forty laps and today, and I took a blood test for a nutritional work out and diet. I look forward to finding out about this. I'm trying to crawl out of this. I'm trying to crawl forward. I realized that I don't know what my little girl looks like. I know what my kid looks like, but not that little girl; that made me really sad.

Thursday, July 26th
• *9:40pm* •

I started to read *Incest and Sexuality* and I started to feel better. I realized that I felt I was losing my mind as a result of the fear, shame and paranoia. I've been feeling like I felt when I first realized I was an incest survivor. After starting to read the book, I was relieved because I saw myself in the book and I knew I wasn't crazy. Reading that book three years ago was easy because I was so detached from my own sexuality. I read this definition of sexuality that was beautiful:

> Sexuality refers to how people feel about their bodies and genitals, how they choose to express sexual energy, and how and with whom they prefer to share sexual feelings. In sexual expression, a woman projects her intimate self

outward. She takes hidden aspects of herself – her genitals and their sensation – and reveals them to herself and perhaps to a partner. (Maltz and Holman, p. 8).

For some reason this made my little girl feel safe and I gave her permission to feel anything. I was only able to see a little girl's vagina and her putting her finger in herself, and I knew it was me as a child, and then I saw an outline of a little girl coming out of the bathroom and I knew she was bleeding, but then the sexual arousal began because the little girl was masturbating and all of a sudden the image of the vagina grew to an adult size and I knew it was me today. I told Lyn about the outlines of this and she said my sexual development stopped at five and a half or maybe it has never started and I need to go through adolescent sexuality and then being an adult. I hope I get a picture of that little girl. I'm going to read some more of *Incest and Sexuality*, but I've decided to skip over the personal stories for now.

Saturday, July 28th

● *7:15pm* ●

I just got a call from that guy Brian from the Saturday night meetings of families of alcoholics. He called to see if I was going to the meeting and if I wanted to go out for ice-cream or yogurt afterwards. We were on the phone for about a half hour. The very little I know about him I like. I called Lyn and told her Brian had called and then hung up the phone and jumped up and down in the middle of my bedroom from joy.

● *12:17am* ●

Just got home. We had a great time. We ate ice-cream (mine was sugar-free) and played three games of pinball, one game of packman, and one game of space galaxy. We talked about schools we attended; he is about four to five years younger than me. My little girl is a little anxious, but really OK. I was able to say just, 'Good night Brian.' He asked if he could give me a hug and I said OK. He's really affectionate and demonstrative. Tonight went really well. I realized my little girl is willing to deal with sexuality issues as long as it's in a safe place. I guess with Brian it's a little bit easier just because he knows I'm an incest survivor from the first meeting we were ever at together three years ago.

Monday, July 30th
• 10:54pm •

I've had some more awareness over the last two days. I realize that I'm afraid to show a guy that I like him or be affectionate because I'm afraid the touching will get out of control and I'll be raped. So, I don't express liking someone or affection and come across as seemingly cold or indifferent. I have no frame of reference of appropriate touching and its sequence, so I do nothing and withdraw.

Wednesday, August 1st
• 10:30pm •

I'm working on a new project at work and not only is it technical, but I have to teach myself Lotus. I'm going to be a computer wiz kid soon. I worked on charts and lotus for five hours today.

I finally got to see Don. He came back from vacation with the beginnings of a beard. He really looked cute. We chatted. He said he's not sure about me seeing him every other week and maybe in two weeks we'd go back to every week, and I said OK since I'm not sure either. I was talking to him about this job thing. He said he's been trying to gear me away from looking for another job. He said my job may not be the best but it has positive sides, such as not being excessively demanding, and I'm making a great salary considering the few number of years I've been working and the fact that I don't have a masters. He said I have other priorities and it's hard to go to graduate school and have a demanding job. So I'm praying for acceptance and crying over the fact that I'm not getting my way.

I told Don about the writing assignment Lyn gave me on 'stinking thinking', and he said he was glad that he wasn't the only one I frustrated and I'm a brat with. He said he hates my thinking; it's crisis ridden, rigid, and failure oriented; if I just trust the process, ask for guidance, trust my feelings, and deal with my sexuality, my life will be manageable. If I don't, it will explode in my face. I told Don about the incest surfacing and he reminded me that it doesn't go away.

He was teasing me about never going on a date. I told him that while he was on vacation I had and that he has to take his foot out of his mouth. He literally put his shoe in his mouth and then started eating the bottom of his pants while I was doubled over laughing on the couch. He said he'd flip his chair over but he will crack his head on the desk since he has rearranged the furniture. He was really shocked that I waited until the middle of the session to tell him. He wasn't thrilled that the guy was from an alcoholic family. I told Don that he was being too pushy, and to give me a break. Sometimes it feels it must be Don's way or no way; that's when I tell him to stop. I remember Don saying during the session that the reason I can't see my little girl is that she is covered in shame.

Wednesday, August 8th

● *6:30pm* ●

I'm so confused. Part of me is really happy and part of me is really sad. Last night I called Brian back; we spoke for about a half hour and he asked me to go to a concert with him on September 1st. When I hung up, I jumped up and down around my room for the second time as a result of this guy and then I got scared. I really like him, but I don't know how to date. I'm going to find out.

There's a part of me that's really sad because I miss my Dad. It seems with every nice event in my life or every change, my father's spirit moves just a little bit further from my reach. I know it's because I continue to grow and live, and with every event it is another thing my Dad isn't here to share with me. This grieving is so difficult.

I realized I haven't written or spoken about this and it's time: My sister, Annamarie, has been working twelve-hour days for four months, and it's finally taken its toll. Two weeks ago, she was visiting my mother and she told her she thought she was manic depressive because she had been thinking she would be better off dead. Today, my sister went to my Dad's doctor and he diagnosed her as manic depressive and believes it biological. My sister is finally at her lowest. I pray she stops drinking, especially as a result of taking this medicine – she's not supposed to drink alcohol with this medicine, but Annamarie is the one with the drinking problem. I hope she gets help.

Thursday, August 9th
● *6:10pm* ●

Prior to entering a recovery program I was:

A workaholic, the family hero both at home and at work, physically and emotionally shut down, enraged, asexual, had an inflated ego to cover my insecurities, no relationship with my immediate family, highly critical, self-reliant, religiously fanatical, not intuitive, living in an active situation, always self-protecting, living in fear which was disguised as hyperactivity, close-minded, believing I was stupid, acting as a martyr or know-it-all with the teens I worked with, rescuing other people, was involved in causes, had no self-image, no body image, no sense of touch, nor intimacy.

As a result of my recovery for over six years:

1 My work is no longer my life, and I've learned how to set boundaries by saying no; but my sense of self-worth is still connected to my job to some degree.

2 I no longer try to save my family or people at work. I try to mind my own business.

3 I am emotionally available. I feel, recognize and can name my

feelings. Physically I am able to stay in my body and not split. I have regained a sense of touch both internally and externally.

4 Most of the time I have no stomach problems. When I do, it is as a result of projecting negatively into the future.

5 Most of my rage at my childhood has been expressed to either Don or Lyn, or through my writing.

6 I know and feel at times that I am a female, but I am still afraid to expose and own this reality. I'm working on it.

7 My ego still gets in the way, but it has been burst many times. At the moment, I am trying to find out what I am ashamed of.

8 I have been able to make amends to my immediate family and am able to have a relationship with them to the extent they're capable of intimacy.

9 The more compassionate and in touch with pain I become, the less critical I am.

10 Having come through the worst aspects of incest, I know I can't do it alone, but sometimes I forget.

11 I needed to be religiously fanatical so as to stay in denial. I have no spirituality, but I do have faith in my recovery.

12 I am trying to stay in today because I only project doom and gloom and fear. I'm not that powerful that I can tell the future.

13 Now I know that when I'm running around, I'm afraid of something, and with the help of Lyn or Don I try to figure out the fear and talk it out.

14 I'm trying to keep an open mind because I didn't even know about my own story, which means I don't have all the answers and I can learn something.

15 I have slowly come to own some of my gifts and talents, and have let go of some of my old tapes. I believe that I am very intelligent.

16 I was out to save all those teenagers and probably wanted

someone to save me. I considered myself a expert on teenagers. I knew how they should live and what their problems were – so I thought. By focusing on them, I never had to get to know myself. I stopped any kind of volunteer work for the past several years to find out what my own beliefs and values are.

17 I only knew the illusion I learned which denied the alcoholic and incestuous family system. I didn't know who I was without this denial, until now.

18 Today I know I'm not huge – I'm not size 16, 6'5", and 300 pounds. Nor was I ever that size. My body image is not totally accurate, but it is close enough for me to buy sizes 10 and 8 in clothes.

19 I have had my sense of touch returned by slowly realizing that I needed nurturing and love and by letting Lyn, Don, sometimes my mother, and friends hold me. I am also learning the difference between sensual touching and affection. I don't have much of a healthy frame of reference of touch.

20 Today I have various levels of intimacy in my life from deep intimacy with Lyn, and Don, to very superficial intimacy like my relationship with Brian. I'm learning that not all relationships are the same, nor do they last forever.

Friday, August 10th
• *10:54pm* •

Last night, I went on my second date with Brian and we played miniature golf. We also kissed, hugged, held hands, and I was able to tell him what I was comfortable with and what I wasn't. I was able to tell him on the way home that I was scared because of all the affection he showed me; and he said he wouldn't touch or kiss me, and he didn't until he asked if he could kiss and hug me good night. We spoke about our families. We spoke about our issues with feelings, sexuality and where our recovery has brought us. I was amazed at how verbal he was about his attraction to me and how gentle and considerate his touch is.

I felt comfortable expressing my fears about dating, touching affectionately versus sexually, and I never once felt defective.

Brian touched me with the exception of sexual areas, and was gentle, sensitive, and whenever I did get scared he just hugged me. His gentleness brought up issues of deprivation, and neglect of affectionate touching, and just made me feel sad because I am always expecting touching to hurt. Just kissing him made my insides melt and I wanted to be closer to him.

Today at work I was stressed out. The only backlash I had was anxiety and waking up at 5:00 am. My body was fine and there was no negative physical recall. This very tall, black haired, green-eyed, gorgeous-legged man is open, honest, and has a gentle soul. I'm moved to tears by his gentleness. I didn't lose control once with him. I only need to reduce the fear. My little girl really likes him but is really afraid to believe in the hope and joy of this person; it's easier to believe in the doom and gloom because it's more familiar than the healing of recovery. I told Brian I was afraid that he would think I was boring, and he said no way. This guy is really attracted to me and the feeling is mutual. I'm trying to be more verbal and express my feeling about him to him, but it's still very hard.

I was telling Alicia about him, and she said I couldn't get this smile off my face. I know I'm definitely 'in like' with this man. We made plans go to Fire Island, Lincoln Center for the outdoor concerts, and the Catskills; I haven't been there since I was a kid. I'm trying to be honest and present and enjoy the moment. I'm proud of the fact that I was able to let him physically close and yet set boundaries which he accepted and respected. I think I'm going to get in touch with some pain though; I feel it surfacing and I need to talk to Don and Lyn because it feels like hopelessness and that's only sabotage.

I realized that I'm afraid to believe in hope and yet there is a spark inside that is trying to catch on fire. I know I want to eventually have sex with Brian. I know I have a sense that some day I'll become a writer and publish my journals, but I'm afraid to believe in these hopes and dreams, so I keep it a secret. I'm afraid to long for something because I'm not sure it will come true. My fear of sexual intimacy is making me compulsive at work and making it very hard to sit still. I'm getting less and less sleep and feeling more stressed. I'm also having a hard time just listening and being open-minded at meetings. I'm afraid that the shame will surface from the bowels of my gut. I'm more afraid of my shame than I am of my sexuality – my shame is repulsive and I will be rejected and abandoned and I'll be all alone again, that little girl who was all alone and ashamed of being a girl. Somehow Brian sees that little girl and tells her it's safe to come out and play with him. The reality is that she is getting the same invitation from Lyn, Don, and my mother to come out and be nurtured, loved, and accepted. I'm sobbing right now because of the pain inside. I need to let go of the shame, which isn't mine and doesn't belong to me. I just got this great idea; I've mentioned touching as a negative, repulsive feeling, because of the incest, but all of a sudden I wanted to write about positive touching I've received. The first person I thought of is Lyn.

Lyn
Sitting on my bed and making time for me to reach out to her for comfort, she was the first person I ever held hands with, sitting in her living room and crying in her arms, having her hold me while I shook from tears or fear, putting my head on her chest and feeling safe, hugging her so our bodies touched, Lyn rubbing my back during a meeting and asking me if she could caress my hair, sitting in my car drinking coffee and five minutes later crying in her lap, or simply reaching out by putting her leg next to mine so I knew she was there while I sobbed.

Don
Hugging him for almost four years at the end of every session and only recently not feeling like a piece of cardboard, hugging him two days before Christmas and he asking me to hug him three times in a row which I obliged, with no feelings, and on the third hug he picked me off the ground and twirled me around, making me laugh, sitting next to me and asking me to hold his pinky finger so I wouldn't go back into the past alone, crying in his lap in agony over my childhood, sobbing in his arms the day I found out my Dad had a brain tumor, he sitting on the edge of

the coffee table in front of me with his open palms facing me inviting me to reach out and connect with him.

Mom

Hugging me three years ago while I was naked in the tub while I sobbed over the realization that I was physically abused and her not knowing what was wrong, lying with my head in her lap and her scooping me up in a snuggle and caressing my hair, sitting with our legs touching on opposite ends of the couch, rubbing my back and rocking me.

Others

Vanessa's hugs that tell me she loves me and I'm safe with her, Jessica who is eight years old and teaches me about affection, my father hugging me, caressing my face, laying my face on his palm, and he caressing my hair.

Sunday, August 12th
● 6:00pm ●

I'm feeling serene. Part of me feels like my date with Brian was a dream. I can't believe I trusted him enough to be kissed, hugged, and caressed, and to talk about boundaries. I was reading some meditation book and I got this realization. You know that sensation when your foot falls asleep; as it regains its sense of touch you have pins and needles. I realize that the day after the date my lips were pins and needles. Not in a painful way, but as if they were coming back to life. I'm opening the door to my sexuality and walking through the door so I can recapture it again in a healthy way. The anxiety I feel is due to wanting to own my own sexuality and owning that realization. In the past I wasn't able to buy clothes that represented me, my sexuality, or my creativity.

Tuesday, August 14th
● 9:25pm ●

I realized that my anxiety is not about my sexuality, but about Brian seeing my shame and being repulsed by the slime.

Last night I saw how toxic my thinking is. Brian left a message for me on my machine; he wanted to talk to me and so would I call him back. I proceeded to smoke my second cigarette and convince myself that Brian was calling me because his friend told him to break up with me so he could keep the focus on himself. And I was able to say to myself, 'I'm disappointed, but I understand that your recovery had to come first and you have to let go of distractions in order to deal with your feelings.' Mind you, this conversation was all in my head. When I did call him back he wanted to thank me for our date and for bringing joy to his week. What a fucked-up perception I have.

The shame is finally starting to seep out because I'm feeling fat and ugly, and yesterday I had a flashback of my little girl bobbing in a sewer system where the abuse occurred trying not to go under. In addition both yesterday and today I smelled sweat and dirt several times during the day and I knew I was having a flashback of my uncle. I hope Brian won't smell like that during sex, if I ever get the opportunity. Tonight I shared and cried about how fucked up my perceptions are and that the last two weeks I've had about ten compliments about my hair, my looks, how good I look in a bathing suit and how thin I am. I wish I saw what others see.

Wednesday, August 15th
• 9:00pm •

The shame is so great within. Somehow Brian's gentleness and our mutual attraction are making me deal with shame. The shame is so painful that it leaks out in droplets. I was sad all day at work and was driven, worked late, and then went food shopping. I got home at 8:15 pm and took a bubble bath and just whimpered in the tub. I can't see my little girl; she's buried alive under the slime, but I can hear her crying. I'm afraid of this pain, I'm afraid of how it will feel to let this shame out. I felt fat and ugly, but I keep getting compliments from colleagues and strangers. I know this shame has nothing to do with Brian, and yet I feel it the most around him. I'm afraid to let him get to know me because he's going to see the slime. I see a little girl with slimy wet stringy hair. This is so painful I'm sobbing my eyes out. My little girl is covered in sewer slime.

Today at work I saw Alicia and started to become tearful, and I told her I was dealing with shame and feeling slimy. She took my arm and walked me into the bathroom and told me to look into the bathroom mirror and tell her what I saw. I told her I saw an attractive lady. She said a pretty lady with great legs, who is thin and dressed nicely. There is no way I could dress this way if I really thought I was slimy she said.

I just read something on shame by Michelle and Artemis in *The Courage to Heal:* 'So to heal shame, you just dive right into that shame and you risk letting somebody love you inside of that.' (Bass and Davis, 437).

I'm going to try. I told Lyn that I want to hug Brian or touch his hair or face, but I can't because I'm afraid he'll reject me. Lyn said the best way to get over that is to just do it unless it gets too scary, then I can just verbalize what I want to do instead of doing it.

Thursday, August 16th
● *10:35pm* ●

I had an interesting session with Don. I told him everything that happened since the last time I saw him. He didn't want to talk about shame. He said it's all about control. I needed the control as a child to survive; if not I'd be dead. But the fact that I hold on to the control today where it's no longer needed means I am therefore perpetuating the incest. Don said I have to find a God and have some spirituality. He said I have all the rage about the God I grew up with, but I just put it on the shelf; holding onto the rage helps me stay in control. He said I need to let go of the rage to make room for spirituality in my life. Lyn said she sees the rage on my face. If I don't let go of the rage, I won't grow. By holding on to the rage, I can rationalize my shame and my fear of intimacy. Lyn suggested I write on my rage towards God.

God

I was told you were an all-loving God, a God who was all powerful and all knowing. If you were all knowing, how could you allow me to be tortured by my uncle? If you were all loving, how could you let him harm my body? If you had anything to do with his death, you were about eight months too late. This monster was my babysitter and you just left me all alone and unprotected. My parents weren't emotionally or physically there and neither were you! Then once my uncle died I was to forget everything, as if nothing happened, and be the good little Catholic girl; except we are considered bad if we have sex before we are married, we are bad if we masturbate, and we are bad if we hate someone who died at seventeen years old.

I was the victim and yet I was the one who got punished. You stupid fuck. God you picked on a little girl. I picked a faith that was a sham, preaching a loving, forgiving God and yet you let my little girl go through that horror. Your fucked up church is so dysfunctional; it was a perfect place to hide from my sexuality because anything to do with sex was dirty – except from the moment you got married, then it instantly became sacred. I tried all my life to be good. I practically lived in your church and when I needed my faith most I realized it was just an illusion, like the illusion that my Uncle Marco loved me. I was betrayed by both of you, except you, God, keep fucking people's heads up with your Catholic rules and regulations. I desperately needed you and you left me all alone. There was no one there for me. A five-and-a-half-year-old little girl in a foreign county, tortured, bleeding and alone. I hate you for what you didn't do. You didn't provide me with protection. You let everyone, including me, believe Uncle Marco was wonderful for another twenty odd years. You left me to die alone. You betrayed my innocent faith in you, and then you continued to be a role model through your church so I could earn absolution for some fucking act that wasn't my fault. My uncle got the hero's burial and I got the shame and slime.

Because of your fucked-up pious rules, I never got to see if my uncle was really buried and dead or if he would come back some day. Everyone noticed when he got hurt, but no one noticed when I got my head bashed on a cement wall, or I was bleeding, or black and blue due to repeated rapes. No one noticed the fact that I couldn't eat, or that my back and torso were beaten. But you made sure that my family was attending to him at the hospital. I hate myself for ever having faith in you.

I'm feeling sad right now because I'm remembering a pseudo-sense of community; when I was in the midst of a Catholic community, but unreachable, no one penetrated the shell and that's where I belonged because I was untouchable. I even lost the illusion of community and came face to face with the fact that I've been alone my whole life until the incest came out. My shame and self-hatred kept me in quarantine, and you continued to do nothing but let things evolve, and yet you call yourself God. I lost my faith in you when I was five and a half, staring out the window knowing I was trapped and it was hopeless, except I didn't know I didn't have a faith until I needed it twenty plus years later. I had Catholic rigidity, bullshit, fear, shame, and emotionalism, but no faith.

Because of what you condoned, I have more faith in doom and gloom than in love and joy. I believe in shame versus humility and I am not free of fear. You shattered everything that was wholesome, pure, innocent, and sweet. You helped create, through my uncle a slimy, brutalized, scared, and enraged little person who knows absolutely nothing of love, affection, wonder, spontaneity, or simply being a girl. And yet I was told you were a loving God. Just get the fuck out of my life and stay away. You have already ruined my childhood, I don't want you or your fucked up Church anywhere near me today.

The only fucking reason I'm even writing about you is that I'm starting to hate myself again, and I might as well hate you and be angry with you rather than continue hurting myself. I think I'm going to use my defiance and fight you out of my life just like my uncle. He doesn't matter any more either.

August 18th
• *3:21pm* •

Today I was on the verge of tears and just stuffed my face by eating pastries and smoking. I went to a meeting and heard something that applied to me. I realized I've held on to this shame all my life and it was within me, almost as if I were sitting on the box keeping it in. But if I let go, all the shame will ooze out and everything will be covered in it. It's one thing to feel the shame from within, it's another to let it out and contaminate everything. Then everyone will know my shame.

Lyn said the shame feels horrible as it is coming up and out, but once it's out, it can be buried in my uncle's grave where it belongs. She said I need to talk to safe people about this shame and by talking about it and absorbing nice experiences into me, the shame cycle will be broken.

Monday, August 20th
• *11:09pm* •

I had a great day with Brian. We went to the Museum of Modern Art and walked around the city. Then we came back home and cooked dinner; he cut and cleaned the salad because I told him he had to help and it was cute to watch him learn to clean salad. He held me up in the middle of the kitchen while I was holding salad bowls in my hands, and was kissing me; he said I had to trust him. I told him I had no choice considering he could drop me on the floor.

Being physical was easier today than last time. I forced myself to touch him and be affectionate. I told myself that if Brian was going to feel slimy he would have to tell me. I was able to tell him that I described him to Lyn as a gentle soul with the best-looking legs in town. It was wonderful and scary at the same time. We went to the meeting where someone was talking about physical abuse and shame and feeling different; afterwards we went to the park for ten minutes and I broke down sobbing and Brian held me. All I told him was that I could identify with everything the guy said, that my pain had to do with shame.

That's when Brian reminded me 'not to pet the monster', meaning not to give shame all this power.

Wednesday, August 22nd
• 7:12pm •

Today was really a great day. Brian was at my apartment at 7:30 this morning to pick up his money that he had left there from Monday. It was really cute. He was totally casual and I was dressed for work. He was really funny. He was amazed at how self sufficient I am, and that I live alone and totally support myself. He said his mother was totally dependent on his father and he's really glad that I'm able to take care of myself. He asked me if I wanted to go over to his place and see a video with him. I told him that I need to just spend some quiet time with myself; he said he's constantly amazed at my honesty. I called him later on today to tell him my mortgage application was approved for my co-op. I'm so excited. I was hyper with joy, and it was nice just to share that happiness.

I keep getting two pictures in my head of Brian while we were out on Monday. One was while we were at the Museum of Modern Art. I saw this painting I loved and wanted to write down the name, but my shoelace became untied for the third time. He asked me if I wanted him to tie my shoelace and I said sure. I assumed that after I'd finished writing down the information, I'd pick up my foot so he could tie my shoe. The next thing I know this man six feet plus, is kneeling in front of me and tying my sneaker! I almost started to cry. No one has tied my shoes since I was four years old. I was so touched by that amount of caring. The other scene is Monday night in my kitchen when I had salad bowls in my hands and Brian grabbed me, and I was suspended in air with glass bowls in my hands and I had to trust him. All I can do is laugh; he was so cute.

I spoke to Lyn and I had some painful awareness. I'm beginning to realize that I want a woman therapist to go through my sexuality with. I realized that my mother was not a role model of what a woman should be; the only woman who has shown me that is Lyn. I realized that I want a woman who is a sex therapist and deals with incest survivors. E. Sue Blume wrote a book on incest, works on Long Island, and Lyn has met her personally. I know it's not time, but I have the awareness that now I need positive female identification in being a woman and dealing with my sexuality, but I need to work out this issue about God with Don. I'm not ready to do anything, but I need to talk to Don about issues of control over my recovery, and once I do that I know that I'll have a better barometer about how to go forward.

Tuesday, August 28th
• 7:25pm •

Last Thursday I totally forgot to talk to Don about the comment he had made last week about my little girl. I had told him I was having a hard time buying any clothes for myself, and he said not to let the shame and slime affect me and to buy something pretty, sexy, and feminine for my little girl – and my stomach turned over. There's nothing sexy about my little girl. For some reason, I forgot to share that his comment from last week upset me. If Don feels my little girl is sexy, we have a problem. I truly don't believe he meant that comment towards my little girl. I think he got my adult and my little girl confused, but I need to clear it up. I realized that my awareness about believing that God is a perpetrator somehow transferred to Don being a perpetrator. I felt him staring at my legs and I don't really know if that was real or if I'm feeling exposed. I really need to clear up this issue.

The other thing is that I need to write about Brian, and that is painful to do. Sunday, Brian had tickets to the Yankee game and we went for two to three hours, and it was nice being together but not having to talk throughout the game. We were comfortable with each other. The nice part is that we were physically connected. I either had my hand on his leg or his fingers were going through my hair. I don't know if it's sexual attraction or just going through adolescence. I was able to tell Brian that having his entire tongue in my mouth when we french kissed is not possible for me to handle right now because I have flashbacks of having my uncle's dick down my throat. I was really scared and filled with shame, but when I finally looked up he was smiling and complimenting me on how honest I am. He came in for a drink of water before going to work and I felt so relieved and happy.

Then yesterday I was at his apartment at 7:30 am and we went to Fire Island and went into all these really expensive shops. We spent five hours at the beach after visiting different sites. We went in the water, he read his newspaper, took a nap, I read the paper while he slept. It's such a nice feeling of being in someone's company that you like and still being totally yourself. It was romantic walking on the beach together, rowing for a half hour, lying in the sun totally wrapped up in each other's arms and legs and it felt so natural.

All these firsts are more fun than scary if I listen to my inner child and let her lead the way. My body just wants to screw the hell out of Brian, but my little girl is not emotionally ready for it.

This morning I woke up with some shakes, but the tears were there too, and on the way to work I realized that the sadness was due to my lost adolescence, my lost femininity, and my lost experiences of sexuality. My teenage girl finally believes that Brian is not going to turn into a monster but is my friend and boyfriend, and if I can't talk to him about things that affect us, then the relationship will die.

I talked to Lyn about Brian and touching. I told her that my body is ready to have sex with him, but his touching is non-sexual for the most part and that is more disarming than sex. I feel more out of control and vulnerable and exposed than just having sex with him. Lyn said the only frame of reference of touching is my uncle and that was violent. With Richard, the only guy I ever had sex with, there was no touching, just sex. So Brian's gentleness and touching makes me feel out of control because they are unfamiliar, so the feelings that are aroused are sexualized because I have that frame of reference. Lyn confirmed my belief that the tears are due to deprivation of touch, and where there is any depravation there is a loss. It confirms that incest affected every molecule of my being.

Friday, August 31st
• 6:00pm •

Dear Marco – You Disgusting Prick

You were absolutely wrong, and everything about you was wrong too. I found out last night that I'm an affectionate person. Brian said that first, and then Mom confirmed it, and Don said it's definitely so. I've viewed myself as a cold fish my whole life and I'm finding out that I'm warm, affectionate, and loving and *I'm not slimy*! I may not always feel slimy-free, but I know I'm not slimy. The more risks I take, the more verbal and demonstrative I become with my affection, the more the slime falls away. Brian doesn't seem to be repelled by me touching him.

So you, disgusting prick, were wrong. I hated touching you because you were slimy, dirty, bloody, and sweaty. Lying in sewer water, I thought I caused the slime to come out of my body, but only pain, blood, sexual responses, terror and rage emerged. The more I let Brian caress me and hug and hold me in non-sexual ways, the more I heal because his gentle touch is slowly replacing the painful memory cells. He's able to see through me and see that little cute girl who is buried under the slime. There's still slime on her that she has to let go of, but there's this cute little impish face that is emerging and her hands and arms are free of shame and she is taking baby steps towards healing. So, you disgusting prick, the incest curse is shattering, as Don says. I'm not letting you hold me back.

I realized I believe that having a boyfriend was like having a noose around my neck, but with the right person he's adding to my life and I'm actually letting go of baggage because people like Brian, Lyn, Don, Mom, Julie, Natalie, Gena, Frank, and Christopher represent reality and were able to see parts of me I wasn't capable of seeing because I was wearing incest–victim glasses.

Even if Brian left tomorrow, I would still have gained so

much. The shame is slowly cracking off of me, and it's due to gentleness and love from myself and from those in my life. So, not only are you losing the battle, you are beginning to lose the war too. And I'm going to help, too. Maybe I had all this pain in order to get all this strength and courage. I can still taste the hatred in my mouth for you, but then I flick you away like a piece of lint and you're not important any more.

Thursday, September 6th
• *6:10pm* •

I took a risk last night. I phoned Brian and told him that I like him, that I cared about him, and that he mattered. He wasn't able to acknowledge it at all at first; he talked about tennis, but when I asked him if he knew it, he said yes because he can tell and because I'm affectionate with him. I also told him he was handsome. He told me he thought I was pretty wonderful and liked dating me. After he said that, I listened. He said that he has been physically intimate in the past, but not emotionally, that he's dealing with issues of abandonment, fear of rejection, guilt, shame, and pain; the only person he trusts is his friend because that's where he can talk about the real issues and not bullshit about sports. He said anybody who is grateful about coming from an alcoholic family is nuts.

I told him that I'd like to touch him more, but I'm afraid to because he would get slimed. He said he would tell me if he was uncomfortable. I asked him if we were still on for Thursday night, and he said he was working and forgot, and he was working all weekend except for Monday. But maybe he could come over after the weekend and kiss me on the lips and pinch my butt. I laughed and said I would love that. He was so surprised that I had responded positively. I also reminded him that I was going to Atlanta with my sister to pick up my other sister's car. He told me to call him when I got back if I wanted him to visit. He said he only trusts his friend, and I must remember what I said about people being in your life for a certain period of time until the lesson is learned.

I got off the phone and went to sleep because it was late, but this morning I had to call Lyn because my head was saying, 'Brian's dumping you.' I knew that wasn't reality, but I wasn't sure what the message was. Lyn asked me what I thought Brian meant, and I said he's afraid of intimacy, that the only person he trusts is his friend, and he wants to date casually. She said he's saying easy does it, and he's physically available and I have to stay in today and accept that I'm infatuated with him but need to let go. She feels I'm getting clingy and expecting Brian to be somewhere he's not. She said I'm rushing and controlling the pace of the process; then she reminded me of something I told her a long time ago. I'd said that when adults from alcoholic families find a good thing, they cling to it for dear life. She said I have to decide if I want to get sexual with Brian, and if that is what I want. She said I need to let go and live my life and not wait for Brian to ask me out. I can invite but not expect. She said this is casual dating, and I need to go out with other guys, have fun, go out with girlfriends, apply to graduate school and then let that go too. She said he's entitled to his feelings and I need to stop trying to control the process. I've known him for five weeks only.

• *10:37pm* •

I have just come home from being with my Mom and seeing the movie *Nobody's Child*. What a difference between seeing it tonight and three years ago! The first time I saw the movie, it was to learn to nurture the child within and get to know her. This time it was a message of hope. She was able to overcome her past and not let it stop her, and she let others help her and love her. I realized that she had flashbacks even when she became totally functional, whole, and had received her Master's from Harvard; and yet it didn't stop her from using her experience of spending twenty years in a mental institution to help others adapt to living outside of an institution.

I realized that what Lyn said to me is true. I feel safer dealing with my past than living in the present or planning for the future. I realized that I'm afraid to hope and believe in my wellness because if I bank on it and live fully, everything may be taken away again as it was when I was a child. Lyn said my uncle is no longer in control of my life; it's time to find another Higher Power. I'm afraid to hope and dream and believe in the power of love, but I need to take that risk because I need to grow.

Sunday, September 9th
• 9:00am •

I'm sitting on Tim and Annamarie's terrace in Atlanta. Vanessa and I are here for the weekend visiting and picking up Annamarie's car, which she gave to Vanessa, and then we're driving straight home tomorrow. It's been great spending time with my two sisters; we relaxed by the pool, watched the tennis match, and just lounged. I'm also smoking and I realized why this morning. I started feeling out of control on Friday, and this morning I woke up feeling like I had electricity through my body. All these sexual feelings are starting to surface and it's scaring me. The conversation I had with Brian scared me because he's having trouble with emotional intimacy but is physically available, and my sexual needs are starting to come over me in waves and I don't know what to do with my own feelings. I don't know what is healthy, safe, and appropriate to do with Brian since he only wants to date casually. I want to jump on him if I listen to my body, but another part of me wants emotional intimacy as well.

My sexual desires are frightening me because they're so strong, and I can see that I'd be more than willing to act on them with total abandonment. I have a funny feeling I would be sexually open and free, just as I am with my feelings if I trust the person. This sense of freedom, of total abandonment, is frightening the hell out of me. All these sexual feelings are making me hyper and I feel I can only keep them at bay by smoking during this weekend or working out during the week until I talk to Lyn and Don. I'm also feeling ashamed about my sexual needs, like I should not feel that way or people will think I'm an easy lay just because I want to have sex.

My need for physical and sexual touch is frightening me; I feel it is as necessary as food and water at this point in my recovery. It's almost like this wild passion is trying to come out, or this monster is trying to come out, and I'm afraid I'll lose everything. If I let go of this passion and let it surface, I'll lose my ability to stop if I get scared, I'll lose my self-respect, and I'll lose everything that is good in my life. My sexual energy is like electricity throughout my body, a force in itself. I feel out of control and out of my element, and I don't know how it's going to change me, or whether it will be for the better.

I remember Don saying a long time ago that sexual drive is the second strongest instinct we have, after survival, and I'm beginning to realize just how shut down I've been all my life, how much of my energy it's taken to block out my sex drive. Right now I feel my body out of control is opposite to my head being in control, and it's scaring me because I don't know what decisions I'll make. I have decided that I won't wait for Brian to come over tomorrow night after driving sixteen hours because I might let my body make some decisions I'll regret. I'll be too tired and too needy to have him stop touching me. Writing all this down makes me feel a little bit more in control.

• 11:45pm •

I'm feeling very anxious and I think it's because I'm going home and I'm going to have to face Brian. I don't even know if we'll date. I feel so disconnected from him; maybe it's because I haven't seen him in two weeks. It's also scary dealing with my sexuality. I'm really frightened of myself, and I guess of Brian in a sexual sense too. I guess my guard is back up so it's hard to trust him; I don't know what I can handle sexually and I don't know what he can handle emotionally. I'm also afraid he might back out of going with me to Gena's wedding, and now I've told them he's going, I'll look like an idiot. I guess I'm feeling rejected.

I'm also feeling ugly and unfeminine. Being around my two sisters this weekend was great and I love them, but I feel so inadequate as a woman. I just don't know what it's like to be whole in that sense. I've smoked all weekend. Right now Anna-marie and Tim are in bed. Vanessa's boyfriend just called her from New York. I'm by myself, trying to figure out if this guy I like is going to be around to date and be a part of my life, at least for now. I hate this process. I feel out of control, stupid, and ugly, and undesirable. The truth is that I'm hurt that Brian pulled back.

I wonder if I'm ever going to find someone where the attraction will be mutual, and go on from there to intimacy. I guess I'm also feeling that I'm doing it all wrong, that I'm too old to learn how to date and flirt and be around men. All my insecurities are back, and I'm tired of all this crawling and climbing through the process. Maybe all I need to do is go home, stop smoking and start talking to Lyn and Don, and hope and pray that eventually I'll get exactly what I need.

Saturday, September 15th

I saw Brian after not seeing him in two weeks and it was nice, but he phrased it the best: 'I feel disconnected because so much time has passed.' Last night, in Don's office I realized how much control has been a part of my life. I control issues dealing with time, dealing with payment. Now that control is crumbling away, I feel a rage starting to build. I'm feeling all this pain of letting go of control. I also realize that I'm yearning for closeness, and my control has always kept me away from achieving closeness with people.

I'm feeling very anxious; anxiety has caught up with me because I've decided to stop running, feel it, and heal. I woke up feeling very sad, and I'm starting to mourn what has been robbed from my life by being in control, or believing I was in control. I'm mourning the loss of closeness and intimacy in my life. I know there were people in my life I could have been close with, but the need to be in control and isolated was stronger than the need for intimacy. I have emotional intimacy in my life, and the beginnings of physical intimacy, and I'm absolutely terrified. The need is as great as the fear, and I'm sad because I'm just starting to see how much I needed to control in order to stay sane in the insanity of my childhood, but the price I paid was so steep. I lost closeness with myself most importantly, with others and even with a Higher Power. I guess letting go of control is making me realize that my uncle was my higher power as a child. But he isn't today, and maybe now I can take that leap of faith and trust a power within the universe. I'm so afraid to even voice this. I'm so afraid of becoming the victim again, but the more my control fails me the more I need a spiritual Higher Power.

I'm trying to believe that this Higher Power is the power of love, like I've found in Lyn, Don, and in my recovery. Lyn said I have that spiritual sense, but I'm afraid to own it and trust it. Brian said that sometimes he hears his Higher Power in music. I said I didn't want to listen to such ideas, and yet the song *Something Happened on the Way to Heaven* has kept playing in my head this past week, and today I finally bought a recording of it. Tonight on the way to the meeting I listened to the song and I imagined my Higher Power singing it to me.

I thought of how I should have died at least twice in my life: when I was born at five months three weeks and weighed only a pound and three quarters and could fit in a cigar box; when my uncle cracked my head against a cement wall. My soul was on its way out, but my Higher Power had other plans. Maybe my Higher Power was powerless over my uncle too, and cried with me and for me. Today, with the tools of my recovery program I have too much recovery to run and hide. I could not run and hide from incest, from being a member of an alcoholic family, or from my Dad's death. Today, I can face things as they happen. I must in order to live. Running and hiding means the incest is still controlling me.

Monday, September 17th

● *10:14pm* ●

I spent the day with Brian in the Catskills. It was really the first Fall day this year and it was crisp. We got up there around 12.30pm and walked around and lounged, then we took a nap in the car from 3:00 pm to 4:30 pm because it was so cold. It was so funny to see Brian on his back sprawled out with his hands behind his head, and there I am in the seat next to him on my side of the car in the fetal position with my hands across my chest. It was really hard trying to nap because even though I know I'm safe, my little girl was afraid she would be molested in her sleep. Later on we were walking and I had my nose in his shoulder and he said I'm like a little puppy. When we got back to my apartment, we shut off all the lights and looked at my goldfish for about forty-five minutes and then we started petting.

Someone at tonight's women's meeting said the healing happens so subtly, and then we get to the point we dreamed of. Suddenly, I got an image of Brian and me; earlier this evening he was lying on top of me, both of us fully clothed, my legs wrapped around him, and he looked down at me and said, 'I wish you would stop attacking me', and I burst out laughing. The feelings that surfaced were so powerful and strong I couldn't stop shaking, and I told him I was scared and needed to slow down the pace. We were physical for about fifteen minutes, but it was all I could deal with.

After the meeting I was feeling sad and I realized why. I'm starved for nurturing, for touch, and I'm much more comfortable getting it from men than women. I don't have any experience of nurturing from women, except from Lyn and I need to tell her that.

Saturday, September 22nd

• *10:38pm* •

I feel right now I'm on a pink cloud. The fact that I'm buying this co-op and that one week from now I will be sleeping in it is starting to sink in and I'm beginning to feel joy. Then Brian came with me to Gena's wedding and it was another first. It was the first time I have ever been to a wedding with a boy-friend. Someone asked me if Brian was my boyfriend and at first I wasn't able to answer, but I did say yes. We danced, and I was flirting with him. That wasn't easy but it was a good feeling, and every time we're together we learn a little bit more about each other. It's going real slow but it's going. After the wedding, I got home and wrote the essay for my application for graduate school and I put that in the mail.

I had to call my mother because I was becoming emotional. I'm finally living my life and doing the stuff I need and want to do. I feel that the tide is finally beginning to turn and the sun is beginning to shine. The amount of love and gratitude I'm feeling at this moment is bringing tears to my eyes. I just looked into my God box and dated the slip of paper pertaining to graduate school with today's date; and now I have to turn it over to a Higher Power and let it go.

I think it's time to close the door on the past, to begin living in today. I'm going to start a new collection of memories and they are going to be the ones I have some choices in. I want to cry with joy.

Monday, September 24th
● *6:16pm* ●

I'm going to be asleep by 7:30 pm. My legs are killing me from all the dancing we did this weekend, but it was fun. The groom's mother nominated Brian and me as the best dance couple at the wedding. I'm still struggling with smoking. I did swim twenty lengths, but I smoked six cigarettes and I need to stop because I'm starting to get sick.

I'm trying to avoid this painful feeling inside, and I don't know what it's about except that every time I spend time with Brian, when I leave I want to cry because of this pain. I still have a hard time looking at him, and I even ignore him at times. The only time I really look at him is when he's driving. I guess I feel vulnerable. The pain comes up after he's gone. If only I could just cry and snuggle next to him. Somehow the fact that he's still around astonishes me. It's interesting, the more he's trusting me with his feelings, the less demonstrative and affectionate he is. We hold hands, kiss occasionally and hug, but nothing more. Somehow he triggers the loss of affection and nurturing, and I realize how alone and lonely my childhood was. He's somehow bringing up inside my abandonment issues with my family. That's something I've been struggling to keep the lid on. The fact that there's someone here for me brings up all the losses of my childhood. I guess I need to face these feelings so that I can stop abusing myself. But, I feel a great deal of shame about this.

Thursday, September 27th
• *10:23pm* •

I shared with Don my feelings about nurturing, affection, shame, and about asking Lyn and my mother for nurturing and affection. I also told Don that I spoke to Brian about all the loss and shame I was feeling. Don said I need to find out where this relationship is going; if we're not going to see each other more often, and talk to each other more often, then I need to date other guys and get my head out of the clouds. I don't want it be that clear because I think I know. Last weekend at the wedding, Brian was less demonstrative than ever before. It could be because we were in a public place, or because the more emotionally intimate he becomes, the more he pulls back physically, or because he's simply not interested in me any longer. I just don't want to lose one more person.

Monday, October 1st
• *11:20pm* •

I'm feeling sad right now. I got an answer-phone message from Brian calling to say hi and to give him a call tomorrow in the morning because he's running errands in the afternoon. I feel disappointed because this relationship is dying fast, and I would have liked it if he was around. I guess it's time for me to go out again and let go of Brian. I would have loved it if it were different. I guess I'm feeling the loss because I'm crying over a guy. I'm going to miss him. I'm not sure that this is ending, but the fact that Brian has a day off and doesn't want to spend it with me is not a good sign. So, I'm letting go.

Sunday, October 7th
• *1:25pm* •

I have just come in from going dancing. What an amazing day I had. It started with having breakfast with Brian at 8:30 this morning. I told him that I was angry at him even though it wasn't his fault; I'd wanted to go out with him more and he wasn't available. This was after I had asked him why he thought I was angry at him, and he'd answered that it was because he's not around.

He said he wants to date very casually because right now everything in his life is unsettled. I said I'm getting double messages from him, and he said he will try to be clearer. He wants to spend time with men and his male friends, and he has been in denial about his feelings and needs to deal with them. I said to me he's like the wind and I understand that his primary focus is his recovery, but I need to go out more and socialize, that my recovery today requires me to go out and live and learn through experience. I told him I wanted to take my kite out of his car and run, but I no longer want to do that, so that's why we're talking. He said I'm the healthiest woman he has ever dated, but he's still obsessed with his old girlfriend 'even though she's as shallow as a teacup saucer'.

The one guy I want to date is very casual to the point of only kissing and hugging me, talking to me once a week, and seeing me once every two weeks. Brian told me he loves me. I know that I matter to him, but not the way I want to matter. I got out of the car and he just hugged me for some time and kissed me twice, and I said, 'Take care.' He said he would call me during the week. I told him he was an excellent guy.

I walked away and wanted to cry, but I didn't. I went to my Mom's house and stayed there for two hours and then ran errands. Between letting go of Brian and missing my Dad, I felt like my insides were like Swiss cheese so I decided to take my kite and go to the beach since it was such a glorious day.

There was an older man on the beach threading his brother's kite and I asked him to help me with mine. I flew the kite so high that it was the size of a small coin in the sky, and I ran out of thread. The wind was so strong that my hands were pulled up above my head. It took me two hours to reel the kite back in. I felt sadness, ecstacy and exhaustion. I even got sunburned. It was such a nurturing thing to do, compared to how I felt.

Later, I chaired a meeting on nurturing, and it was so good to hear that other people struggle with this issue, that the need is so great for others as well. I was able to see the great strides I've made in my recovery. I got a little emotional towards the end because I felt so vulnerable. Then I went dancing with two women from the meeting and I just danced all night; it was wonderful.

In this crowded bar a man passed by who took my breath away. He passed by three or four times and the last time he put his hand on my shoulder while he waited to go by, and I stuck my hand out and introduced myself and the two women I was with. I bought a drink while he was talking to them. He came over again and put his hand on my back to get by, and then came back and asked me for a pen and gave me his home number and I gave him mine. He said he was going with his friends to another club and asked us to go. I wasn't driving so I said nothing, but the driver said we might meet them later. He turned round to me, and I said I'm not driving so I can't make that decision. He said if he didn't see me later, he'd call me. I was amazed that this gorgeous man had come over to speak to me, and had even exchanged numbers. Tricia said she knew he liked me because he kept staring at me while he talked to his friends, and I smiled at him every time he came by. This is absolutely unbelievable. I can't believe there's a part of me that is becoming approachable and open. This guy absolutely took my breath away. I know I'm getting better.

1991

Thursday, October 3rd
• 12:10pm •

I called Lyn because I was feeling anxious about going to the doctor. I was scared. We were talking about the lesson learned from this near fatal car accident and she said it was to gain spirituality and gratitude. If I'm ever in a similar situation, I can say it's not as bad as this time. She also told me that she has her business cards ready and has office space as of last Friday. I almost started to cry; I was so happy for her. During our conversation I told Lyn that as a result of seeing Julie as a full-grown woman last weekend on retreat, for the first time I saw myself as one as well. Lyn said sometimes we're only able to recognize ourselves when mirrored through someone else. So I've finally grown up. I feel empowered and I think part of that is gaining or feeling a sense of spirituality.

Thursday, October 10th
• 11:25pm •

The week is almost over and I'm grateful because I'm so tired. I have caught up in school. I'm still amazed at what little self-confidence I have. I was up to date with school work. Last week was my first class after being out sick the week before and I asked if I could borrow the notes from someone. No one volunteered. Finally this guy said that if I went to the library with him, he'd let me copy them. Meanwhile, another guy who is in both of my classes stares at me but not in a leering way – he's just attracted to me; there's something I like about his eyes; they radiate warm and fuzzy feelings inside. Anyhow, this same guy doesn't even volunteer to help me. All he says is that he'd be overwhelmed if he ever missed the first day of school.

Tonight, this guy is in my class again and he smiles at me and I find out that his name is Mel. After class he walks me out the door and I realize that the reason why he didn't give me his notes is because he's so shy. If I become friends with him, which I hope happens, when I get comfortable I'll ask him why he didn't offer his notes. I thought he was in his early thirties, but he's a little younger. He's so ordinary – polyester pants, shy, awkward, intelligent; he wants to be a teacher. There's something about him that makes me feel safe. Maybe it's knowing that he's as shy and awkward as I am. I realized that he's taller than I am. I'm going to work on being friends. I realize that the men I've loved, both Christopher and Don, are also gawky, in their own adorable ways.

Sunday October 13th

● *11:47pm* ●

Last night I went out with friends to a jazz club, and we were out until 3:30 this morning. I wore a lycra jump-suit with a belt, and boots; you could really tell what my shape looked like and I looked thin. Five guys came up to talk to me or asked me to dance. I was in such a great mood, had no plans of meeting a guy and was just out having fun. One guy said Tricia and I were really attractive because all these guys were falling at our feet. Then we met Ken who was a friend of Wanda, Tricia's friend; he's an artist and would like to sketch Tricia and me. He kept complimenting us on our legs, and teasing us about modeling for him in the nude, lingerie, etc. We had so much fun, laughing, kidding around, and just flirting. After much coaxing, I agreed to be a model with Tricia in his studio. He told me not only did I have great legs, but I had a great body 'from an artist's perception.' That was when I turned bright red. I told him thanks, but I just wasn't used to such direct compliments. I was amazed that some-one found me that attractive, and could verbalize it. I had gone up to another guy earlier that evening who I had been staring at and I introduced myself. I soon found out that he was shallow even though his looks were great. Ken on the other hand was shy and short, but as we talked to each other, I liked him more and more. I'm thinking I'm finally giving myself permission to be a sexual woman, while still keeping my sexual boundaries.

Monday, October 14th

• *11:47am* •

I'm still having backlash from my own sexuality and being found so attractive. I'm scattered all over the place and can't seem to settle down. I feel like a skittish colt. I called Lyn today, finally, after not talking to her for several days. I realized that I'm afraid to deal with men, flirting, dating, etc. I lose my balance, and just want to run away. Over the past few days I didn't call Lyn, I forgot to pray, and just remained scattered. So I made two phone calls and I am writing again. Although I'm having backlash, I had a wonderful time Saturday night. It was such a good feeling to be able to be relaxed in my own body, know that I looked attractive and sexy, and just be happy whether I meet some guy or not. I called a person in the recovery program and she helped me to realize that I'm dealing with positive anxiety and that I was doing great. She reminded me that I hadn't said yes right away when Ken asked us to model for him. I had said, let me think about it. She reminded me that I took big steps Saturday night. She also reminded me that I'm special because I'm a survivor, that people recognize my inner strength as well as my outward beauty.

• *10:44pm* •

I got on my knees and thanked God. Tonight I told Don about my week. When I told him about my body and knowing I had a nice shape, and then told him about how relaxed I was this past weekend, he told me that I had just integrated my sexuality. So I gave myself a round of applause. I then told him about Mel, the guy in my class, and that I thought he might be a nice guy and I would overlook the fact that he wore polyester pants. When I told Don about Ken and I asked him if Ken was inappropriate; he asked me what did I think? It's not as if he asked me to pose nude, Don said. So I told Don that Ken had done that, and we had told him we wouldn't do it. Don became very serious, and he said, 'Yvette, why don't you see the danger in the situation?' I told him I saw a little of it. Don said that Ken was hiding his wants behind being funny. Don asked how I would feel being stared at for an hour and a half, knowing that this man is fantasizing about my body parts. Don said he wouldn't want a strange woman staring at his crotch. That's when I turned white. I realized I had been skittish out of fear of this guy who had reminded me of a perpetrator. Don said I had just integrated my sexuality; I don't need it to explode in my face.

I also told Lyn, and she said that I have to pay attention to my gut feelings, not laugh things off that make me feel uncomfortable; I can say, 'I don't think this is funny.' Don had asked me why don't I see the danger, and I told him that I'm still amazed that guys find me attractive and sexy. Don also said I need to listen to my own sense. I asked him what I would have done if I didn't have him to talk to; he said I would have realized this all on my own. I feel calmer than I have in days.

Saturday, October 26th
● *6:27pm* ●

I feel like I'm writing less and less because my life is fuller and busier. On Thursday I drove Mel home, like I have done for the past month. I have been so awkward and nervous around him; I kept on repeating myself. This time he leaned over to kiss me, but I said goodbye so he pulled back and got out of the car; then he turned round, got back into the car, said 'What the hell' and kissed me. I just burst out laughing. He looked at me to make sure I was OK, and then got out of the car and left without saying a word.

Last night was our first date. We held hands and walked with our arms around each other's waists. We went to see *Dead Again*. It was a suspense movie and I told him that I sometimes have nightmares. He had his arm around me at the point in the movie when I got really scared; at the end I was really shaking and he said 'Pal, are you OK?' I drove him home and after kissing him for a little bit, I told him I'd call him during the week. He looked at me straight in the eyes, and said that he could easily fall for me. I put my face in my hands and told him not to say that; he was scaring me. He said I was right and I saw his face close up before me. I felt bad because I had told him how to feel. The reason he scared me was that he seemed able to verbalize his feelings so easily. I kissed and hugged him and mushed up his hair and told him I knew exactly what he meant.

Today, Mel called while I was out to make sure I had no nightmares from the movie and to thank me 'for a lovely and magical time.' When I came home last night, I couldn't express what I was feeling, I was feeling very moved, happy, and sad. When I told Lyn, she said she really liked the fact that Mel was so expressive. I asked Lyn if I could fall in love with a guy in a month. She said maybe not fall in love, but definitely clear the path for it. We were waiting to go into the movie and Mel takes my hand and kisses it. He said he always wanted to do that. I feel really safe and comfortable with him, and I feel like I've known him for a long, long time.

Monday, November 11th
● 11:36pm ●

I had a real painful session with Don. When I was talking about Mel last week, I realized my focus had shifted because I used to talk about Don. I told Don that I felt I was letting go of him, that I didn't want to just because I was dating a guy I really liked. Then Don used the therapeutic term 'cathexis', which means that a libidinal focus had shifted. He said that by directing that attraction outward, I was getting ready to leave therapy. I told him I already knew that. Don said he's having a hard time letting go too, that he talks about me to other clients without breaking my anonymity, and that I'm a woman of courage and that he's very proud of me. I'm one of the few incest survivors who hadn't left a recovery process before its completion.

I'm sobbing right now because I know that he really cared about me all these years, that I really love him. Without Don I wouldn't have met such men like Mel. God, thank you for putting me on the path that led me to Don's office over five years ago. Don said I've really integrated my sexuality. I told him that I don't know if Mel is it, but even if he isn't, I'm it. I trust my perceptions and my gut. I'm exhausted from crying. Good night Don – I love you. Thank you for being the balm for my wounds.

Wednesday, November 20th
● *7:53am* ●

I've decided to take a personal day and call in sick. I just needed time to regroup, sleep, and just stop racing. I just read my journal since September. I feel scattered and it's coming out in my writing. I'm not concentrating, I'm not focused. After calling in sick, I got back into bed and this little voice said everything feels out of control. I realized this morning that I'm feeling a lot of fear because so much is going on and I'm feeling overwhelmed. Part of the problem is that I've been racing and my sleep had been inconsistent. I'm also doing new things at work, and I get really anxious when I don't know how to do something.

I feel like I'm going to get found out. Part of it is that Mel doesn't know about my past, another part of it is the conflict of my sexual needs and listening to my inner child. Sexual deprivation is really coming into focus; and yet my little girl freaks out; she gets really scared and is afraid of covering Mel in slime, or making ugly faces during sex. Part of the problem is that I'm projecting, and my fears and insecurities are coming out.

It's overwhelming to have a man who likes me as much as Mel does. I talked to Don and he said this is new and it's hard. I've never been in a relationship like this before. He said it sounds like I'm infatuated and it's reciprocated. I told him I've been running around and I'm exhausted. I told him I have been listening to my little girl and going slowly, but she's really scared and doesn't like this. Don said my adult likes being in this relationship. He said I need to stay with my feelings and write about them. I haven't been doing too much of that. I must stay in the relationship and not sabotage it. I must stop running around, try to slow down.

I told Don that I don't know how to do this, that I have forgotten. The truth is that I'm afraid. I'm afraid of not being in control. All this anxiety is fear. So here I am crying, writing, and reaching out. I knew I was in trouble when I went food shopping and almost bought honey, nearly convincing myself I could eat it. Talk about denial and sabotage! I realize that though my body and hormones are reacting to sexual neglect and deprivation, my deep emotional and physical attraction to Mel is terrifying.

After being physical with him for forty-five minutes I had begun to shake. So I just put my head in his lap and let him hold me. All this is going on in my car. I joked with him that we're too old to be petting in a car, but it's OK for now. I am taking little steps and the relationship is slowly becoming sexual. Last night when I had no clothes on, I felt fat, and I thought that Mel is going to hate my body. My perception of self had changed because as we were moving toward sexual intimacy I rejected myself, felt ashamed of my sexual needs and desires, and needed to view myself as ugly.

Monday, November 25th
● *11:34pm* ●

Tonight I was talking to Don about Mel's sexual past and how that brought up my own incest issues. I also described what I felt about Lyn moving away, that I was a burden. Don said the 'cathexis' shifted with Lyn as well; Mel's the center of my attention now. I said that I feel like a burden to Mel too because of my incest issues that he doesn't even know about. I realized why I felt like a burden. I realized that my little girl felt like she was a burden because she was sent to Italy, a place where none of her needs got met and she was treated as worthless and abused.

Now that my needs are being met, it brought up all that sadness and loss because I realize that I'm not a burden, that I have more love in my life today than ever before. Don said I haven't been loved this intimately and unconditionally by anyone since before going to Italy and I'm mourning everything I've missed. Mel just loves and accepts me physically, emotionally, and spiritually and keeps telling me we have plenty of time. I'm furious at my uncle because he said I was unlovable and he's wrong – Don agreed.

As usual Don was wonderful; he just held me and let me cry. I asked Don why childhood incest was surfacing now. He said it's because I'm finally realizing that getting my needs met isn't burdensome to others; people like Lyn, Don, my mother, Mel, actually just love me because of me.

Thursday, November 28th

On Tuesday Mel and I had a date because he was leaving to go home for Thanksgiving. I didn't get home until 1:30 am and I had to go to work the next day. Mel came over and we had pizza and I gave him a tour of my apartment. Then we went to see *Beauty and the Beast*. This man is so gentle and sensitive. We then went to his apartment. We started talking and kissing, and after a while Mel touched my breasts under my sweater. As soon as we stopped, I started to shake and told him that I was getting scared, and that this had nothing to do with him and could he just hold me. He said 'Gladly.' Then I told him we could resume but that if I got scared, would he stop. He said, 'Yes.' I then made him promise me. He looked me straight in the face and said, 'I understand the meaning of the word no.' I put my head in his arms and started to cry. Then I kissed and hugged him, and I told him that if I stopped I didn't want him to think I was a tease. He said, 'I don't think that.' I asked him why and he said, 'That's not the person you are.' I told him that I was falling in love with him and he was creeping into my heart. He said, 'You just zoomed straight to my heart.' He said he knew it was hard for me to tell him that, but he was glad I was able to tell him how I felt.

Mel's telling me he understands the meaning of the word 'no' meant more to me than when he tells me he loves me. He was more in control of the situation than I was. I had my bra half on and half off, and I pulled off my shoulder pads and told him to take my sweater off but to leave my bra on. He stopped me and asked if I was ready to do that. I realized I wasn't because I said, 'What if you think I'm fat?' I realized I wasn't ready to be half naked. So I told him not to move and I would touch him. He's so gentle and sensitive. He closed his eyes and outlined my face with his hands and said this is how he would feel me if he was blind. He said he's so glad he's not. We're moving really slow, but it's OK. I love the way his body and legs feel.

Thursday, December 5th
• 11:29pm •

The hair on the back of my neck is standing up because I see God's hand in my life. I went to see my graduate advisor for the first time. She wanted to know how I started writing and why I decided to get an MA in creative and technical writing. I told her I'm an incest survivor and wanted to write about the recovery process. She got up and said she had a present for me. She handed me a literary review for which she's the editor, and pointed out an article about the writer, Edith Wharton, and explained how her writing reflects the strong possibility that she was also an incest survivor.

Then, my professor tells me that she wrote a critique on this woman's critique, that she herself is a psychoanalytical literary critic. I started to shake. Here is a feminist, psychoanalytical literary critic who is my professor this semester, and my graduate advisor. I've just found my thesis advisor! This woman is a feminist, happily married, and is interested in psychology and writing. She says she would like me to teach. She said I'm a beautiful person both in and out and people are attracted to me. I can't believe all this good stuff is happening to me. Developing my writing skills, having a boyfriend, and working on my thesis all in one school.

December 9th
• 11:42pm •

Now I know why I was tearful yesterday while I was staring at Mel, knowing that I love him. Tonight in therapy with Don I spent the whole time crying. I realize that because I love Mel, Don is slowly drifting away. I cried throughout the session and I shared with Don how important he has been to me. I realize that I've loved Don for the last three years. Yes, I've had sexual attractions and fantasies about him, but beyond that I told Don that 'I like everything about you.'

I truly love him. Don was the first person to ever see my worst sides and still accept me. He was loving, nurturing, but firm with that little girl who was a brat. He never gave up on me no matter how much I pushed him away. He was able to see the potential in me. Don was loving, consistent, and nurturing without ever being inappropriate. He was there for all the hardest times in my life. He taught me the beauty of men, and I learned how to see them as positive people. I even like his sense of style now. If it weren't for Don, and Lyn, I would have killed myself. I like the way he smiles, his sense of humor and his ability to love and care so deeply.

But, the more I fall in love with Mel the more I let go of Don. I cried the whole session because I'm losing a love as well as a friend. Don asked me when I see therapy ending, and I said sometime in the Spring and he agreed with me. It will be six years in April that I have been in therapy with him. Don said I'll always have a part of him in my heart and me in his. He said when he's going through painful times with other incest survivors, he thinks of me and feels hope for other clients. He said letting go is hard for him, too, and if he needs to he will talk to Martha about me and the separation process. I'm exhausted. I had no idea I had such strong feelings.

Sunday, December 21st
● *1:15pm* ●

It's amazing what a half-hour conversation with someone who knows you inside out will do. I've been listening to that little girl inside who is afraid and ashamed of sex and not writing my feelings down. Last Sunday, Mel and I were on the bed. All he had on were his boxer shorts, and I had my pants on. I felt him and the adult wasn't scared. I thought, this penis can't hurt me, and he put his hands inside my pants and was touching me, and I got scared and told him to take his hands away, and I started to shake. Mel said that all I have to do is tell him that I'm scared and he'll stop. I was shaking with excitement and he asked me if I was cold. My body just wanted to melt into his. My breast ached, my vagina wanted him in me and then I became scared of my own sexual desires and awakenings. I was touching his body and feeling his penis in my hand and it was hard and I didn't know if I was holding him right or not, and I went from feeling sexually excited to sad; we had to stop fooling around because I was frightened.

For the next two days I was tearful; I realized that I'm amazed at his self-control. Lyn said of course he has self control; not everyone is like my uncle. Also, my physical times with Mel had made my body more sexually alive and responsive than ever.

It took me six days to realize all this, and during the week I acted out by flirting with Tom at work. I've had no food in my apartment for a month and I've been running away from my feelings. There's a part of me that wants to leave this relationship because I'm afraid. Lyn said I may have to slow down. I may be moving too fast. She also suggested that I talk to Mel pretty soon about the incest. I admitted to Lyn that my adult sexually wants Mel and wants to know all about him, then the little girl is afraid of his body just because he is a man and has a penis. I don't flirt with Mel. I'm afraid to because he'll either think I'm a tease or will lose control and attack me. I need to talk to him about the incest.

Lyn said that I need to respect my limitations without letting my little girl run my life by running away because she's afraid of intimacy, men, and sex. I need to learn not to take sex so seriously. Lyn says think of sex as adult play; not serious and intense. She said I felt like that because of my past and because of the media. So, I'm going to accept my limitations. I'm going food shopping tonight and I'm trying to slow down. Lyn said accepting my limitations for today doesn't mean failure, but growth. I'm going to learn about intimacy, I'm going to learn about how Mel deals with limitations. Lyn said this is definitely frustrating, but I need to accept my limitations for now without letting my little girl win. Part of me still thinks that Mel will be disgusted when he knows I'm an incest survivor. I'm going to really try not to abandon myself. Lyn suggested that I write down things as they happen so I don't stuff my feelings like my little girl wants me to. This dating and sex stuff is difficult; but it's also fun.

Monday December 23rd

● *12:27am* ●

I had a wonderful day with Mel. We went into the city to look at all the Christmas decorations, FAO Schwarz, Rockerfeller Center, ate hot dogs and pretzels and went to see *Father of the Bride*. Then we went back to Mel's house, read the *New York Times* together with my feet under his legs. When the *Grinch Who Stole Christmas* was on TV, I watched it with my head on his lap and him rubbing my back. We talked about fashion, food, books, things we had in common.

It was such a great day to share with the person you love. But then I started to shake when I was lying on his lap. The love and intimacy is sometimes frightening. We were able to only kiss and hold hands and he wasn't all over me. I'm learning about my limitations and being intimate in non-sexual ways.

December 25th

● *11:04pm* ●

What a beautiful Christmas I had. Annamarie and Tim were in. I was so glad to see them. I miss Annamarie so much. We spent Christmas Eve and today together with my entire family and I slept over. Right now, I'm falling asleep and fantasizing about having sex with Mel. I got a CD player from Vanessa, and I set it up and it sounds great. I had a great Christmas. I either saw or spoke to everyone I'm closest to including Don. I spoke to Mel tonight. I started working on my term paper and he called because we're going out tomorrow night. I realize that we are very slowly becoming intimate. Sometimes I'm afraid that we'll get boring. Actually, I'm afraid of the intimacy. God, I pray that Mel can deal with the fact that I'm an incest survivor, and hope that he's not HIV positive. I'm realizing that this intimacy has to develop to withstand these painful situations. I realized I'm terrified of sexual intimacy.

1992

It's four days into January and this is my first entry. First of all New Year's Eve was very powerful. Mel and I went out to dinner and then we came back to my house, and we sat across from each other hugging each other's feet and listening to the soundtrack of *Beauty and the Beast*. It was very hard, but I finally told him about my Dad being manic depressive, and my uncle being my caretaker, and that I was raped and severely beaten at the age of five and a half and this happened throughout the time I lived in Italy. I told him that I had no memory of it until four years ago. I told him about wanting to write about incest, about wanting to kill myself, but not doing so because then my uncle would have won. I told him of the time I couldn't tell anyone because my uncle threatened to kill everyone in my family. I told Mel that I wouldn't let him speak while I was telling him because I had his attention, and I was afraid he was going to leave once he found out that I was an incest survivor.

Mel said I couldn't get rid of him; I was stuck with him. I asked him if he had any questions and he said no and then he said 'I hate someone I've never met', and we just hugged each other for a very long time. We listened to CDs and brought in the New Year together.

Mel slept over for the first time and that was another big step. He was so adorable. Last time we were together I got scared about feeling him and touching his penis, and then I asked him not to take off his pants because I felt we were moving too fast. This time he asked me if I wanted him to sleep with sweats on. There I was in my red bra and panties and I knew I'd be OK with him in his boxer shorts. I wore my Christmas undies for him.

It's amazing the difference it makes trusting someone during sexual contact. Here we were, totally naked, and I knew I was absolutely safe with this man. I was able to touch his penis and touch it when it wasn't hard. I still haven't looked at his penis when it's erect. I'm kind of scared about that. But it was nice waking up next to this warm hairy body whose face I love to look at, whose voice I love to hear, and whose hands are so gentle.

I loved having my legs wrapped around him, my hair covering his face, him watching me, laughing together, and sharing how each other's touch feels. Finding out things about Mel that only I know. The way he kisses my body and says 'Hello' a lot just to check in with me. I'm so grateful that we're both going through this together.

Wednesday, January 8th

• *11:00am* •

I called in sick because I'm physically and emotionally stressed out. I may have had a stomach virus, but not for the last nine days, and I've been nauseous but not able to throw up. Last night when Lyn asked me if it was this sexuality stuff, I had an image of my little girl sitting in a corner with her head between her knees crying, and I just started to shake in fear. I realized I haven't been paying attention to my feelings, but rather to my sexual drive. It feels so wonderful to have someone touch me and be sexually aroused that it's all I've been focusing on. Since I couldn't hear or sense the fear of my child, I was having flashbacks of being forced to have oral sex with my uncle's penis down my little girl's throat. I realized I'm afraid of Mel's erect penis. To me it represents a knife ready to tear me open. I'm exhausted because physically it's like I've had a stomach virus for nine days, but I don't know how much is physical or how much is emotional. I know that I must look at his penis and touch it while it's erect, so that I can get over some of this fear. I have to remember that this will get easier in time. All Don kept saying was, 'Listen to your feelings.' I'm trying to, without letting my little girl run my life.

Don has just called me back and I told him my thoughts. He said that I need to tell Mel what is going on, tell him that I'm scared of his body, his penis especially, in a nice way and ask for his support. I asked Don how fair is it to say to Mel, 'Please feel free to touch my body, but I don't want to touch yours because I'm afraid of your penis.' Don said in the long run it's not fair, but for now I need to ask for his support and help. Don said Mel needs to know what's going on. Don said I've taken two major leaps since I last saw him. First, I told Mel my story and then we slept in the same bed for the first time. Don said I have to move slowly, and Mel has to know what is going on. I told Don I don't want to miss work or start having nightmares again. He told me I was projecting awfulness. I asked Don if I could tell Mel this stuff on the phone, and he laughed and said, 'How non-intimate! You go to bed with the guy and now you want to talk about this stuff on the phone? Your shame is coming back.' So, it's two steps forward, one step back.

Sunday, February 2nd
• 1:01pm •

I had a major slip, I ate sugar for the first time in over a year and it's all to do with my sexuality and letting go of control. Mel stayed over Friday night after we had been to dinner and to see an off-Broadway play. Once again, like last weekend, we were really tired and just held each other and fell asleep.

I woke up in the middle of the night wide awake and ready for sex. Mel continued to sleep for another hour and a half and I watched him. When he woke up, we started fooling around. I let him take the initiative, and I told him that I needed to give him time to explore my body so I wouldn't be nervous. It was another way to let go of control. Don said that there's usually one person who is more assertive than the other but that it can't always be like that, that we need to take turns at times, that if not, I'll be controlling in my sexual relationship as well. When I spoke to Lyn, she said it seemed like a wait and see situation. I may need to remain in control and continue to build trust or I can let go of some control.

We spent half of Saturday in bed and I was not able to have an orgasm. Initially, I thought it was due to how Mel was touching me, but that wasn't the case at all. He explored my body more than ever before. His gentleness, sense of humor, shyness, and caution disarms me. We were fooling around a lot and neither one of us were able to reach an orgasm and we tried on and off for hours. As I was seducing him – I told him that I need to enjoy the moment because my libido is on overdrive. It's trying to make up for lost time, but I can't. It's not fair to myself or Mel. We were making love and I came real close to having sex with Mel. The tip of his penis was right at the threshold of my vagina and I had situated myself that way. I realized what I was doing and stopped. I was really sexually frustrated so I took the risk; I asked Mel to hold me while I masturbated. I was able to let go and lose control and find relief.

After I was finished I put my face in his neck and started to shake, I felt so vulnerable, even with the man I love. It brought up sheer terror and all I could do was shake. I ran around all afternoon after I'd dropped Mel off, and I didn't allow myself to face the fear of letting go of control, how close I came to having sex without a condom. The other cause of fear is the level of intimacy we are entering. I'm in bed and I was thinking of Mel when he called. I was able to tell him I was having backlash because I was amazed at how open I was with him.

Just by talking to Mel a little while ago and sharing my fear with him made me fell better. I'm still tired, but part of that is the sugar in my body.

I told Lyn about my eating sugar, and she said it sounds like I'm not taking my past into account. She said all she hears from me is talk about sexual performance. She said why do I need to have sex with Mel every time he sleeps over? I told her we were both not able to have orgasms because we were probably trying too hard. She said stop worrying and deal with the moment. She said I need to focus on my feelings while I'm touching Mel. I realize I'm very aware of my senses because that is an area that's been so deprived.

After talking to Lyn I started to beat up on myself for eating sugar, for rushing this relationship on a sexual level, and not trusting in God to heal me in this relationship. I need to let go of sexual performance; I realize that I'm rushing the process so I can prove that the incest has no power over me any longer. Instead, I've put pressure on myself and Mel, and negated my little girl inside. I'm glad I took that risk with Mel; the way he loves me just moves me. He's so sensitive and gentle, and I realized this morning that my knees and elbows had been hurting me not because of the cold, but from bodily recall due to incest. I woke up this morning with my hands above my head and my vagina ready for sex, but it was the body of a six year old – I was having a flashback.

So I'm turning over my sexuality to God. I'm going to accept that I'm constantly aroused and just trust that I'll have sex when it's meant to be. I'm trying not to sabotage this relationship. I told Lyn that I came really close to having sex with Mel and I told her I got really upset because I was the one who positioned my body to have sex with him without a condom and his final HIV test results haven't come through. Lyn said I can't take all the blame; Mel has a voice and he could have stopped me as well. Lyn said that I need space to think, to slow down. I also realize that I'm so tired because all this is so emotional. My sex drive alone is exhausting, and so is being vulnerable, not to mention calming down this little girl inside. The more I let go of my will (I have no choice), the more I become aware of what a special person Mel is.

Thursday, February 13th

• *10:29pm* •

So many realizations: on Sunday Mel and I went to the Met and we walked around, talking, laughing, taking pictures, hugging and being close. He hugged me a lot publicly and I kept hiding myself in his neck and playing. I took a whole roll of pictures of us, and when I got the pictures back I realized two things. I realized that I have a hard time receiving all of Mel's love, tenderness, and desires; it makes me feel vulnerable and out of control. So instead I become that little girl who snuggles and hides. When I told Don this, he agreed I was hiding, and he reminded me that I don't need to hide from Mel. He said Mel is not my uncle. He said my uncle was a narcissistic bastard, who mauled and maimed a five-and-a-half-year-old little girl, a little girl who didn't know if she was going to live or die. Today, I don't need to be in that much control. Today, I can let Mel visually desire me and appreciate my body because his aroused state won't hurt me. I shared with Don how hard we'd tried last time but neither of us achieved an orgasm. Don said we need to ask, 'How does this feel?' 'Does this feel OK?' I started to cry when Don said that. I felt my shame rising, and this wouldn't be so hard if I wasn't an incest survivor. Don said, 'You're learning about sex and making love. Anyone can fuck, but there aren't too many people who have good sexual relationships. You're learning about it.'

Friday, February 21st
• 9:13pm •

I'm so tired due to stress. My jaw is sore because I've been clenching my teeth in my sleep. I've also had the runs the last couple of days. It's all because today Mel's second HIV test result came out negative. We started talking about incest, and I said if he had any questions to please ask me. That's when he told me that he started reading *The Courage to Heal*. When he said that, I felt a sense of hope; I felt he would understand me better and also realize I wasn't rejecting him. My little girl stopped running scared and felt safe. She felt understood, and accepted, and loved. All of a sudden I really felt sure that the incest wouldn't win. Now I had Mel on my side to fight the battle. Mel said he did have a question. He asked if I needed to be in control sexually in order to feel safe? because he had noticed that was an issue in our relationship. I told him, Don had pointed out that I was being the controller sexually, and I needed to let go and let Mel take the initiative sometime. I told Mel that once I realized that, I tried not to be so assertive, to either meet him half way or let him take the initiative totally. I was very honest with him. My little girl has been frantic since Monday when he said he was getting tested for HIV. Tonight while talking to me, Mel told me his second HIV test was negative. I really love this man.

February 24th

I'm feeling sad right; now I guess I have little faith or my denial has totally shattered. This incest stuff is very powerful and I forgot how long it has ruled my life. It hurts to know that now it affects Mel too because my fear carries over to him. I finally told him what a handsome man he is and that I love looking at his face. It was really nice last night because all we did was kiss and hug after dinner which consisted of his famous hamburgers and before that we laughed with his roommate. I have wonderful, beautiful times with this man. I think I want to spend the rest of my life with him, and then the incest hits and I'm afraid of this gentle man who tickles my toes and gently moves the hair away from of my eyes, the same man I'm in love with.

Now that I know Mel is not HIV positive, the relationship has become more real; I've come out of denial about incest and relationships. Right now I want to cry – I don't know how I'm going to get from loving this man, but feeling fear about sex, to being sexually free, open, and responsive. I don't know if I have the courage any more. It's been such a uphill battle, and I feel like I'm out of fuel. My fear seems stronger than my courage. I have tons of homework to do, so I needed to write this down and cry. I know I'm assuming that I have to do everything; maybe this is an exercise in faith in God and trust in Mel. Lyn said I must make sure I don't focus just on the sex; I'll sexualize the relationship and I could wind up jeopardizing it. I told Mel yesterday, while I was sitting on his lap, that I couldn't understand how I could ever be afraid of him when all I see on his face is gentleness and love, and yet I get afraid.

I told Lyn and she said that what I'm going through is normal because being in a relationship is new. Even though it's healthy and desired, it will kick up incest issues, but they will settle in time. My feelings won't be like this forever. I told Lyn I guess I have to start having faith in God and trusting Mel. She said I have it backwards; I need to trust God and then myself. If I trust Mel without trusting myself, I'm setting up a situation to be incested. Lyn said I need to listen to my limitations, not forget where I came from. She said that if I let Mel sleep over, I'm asking for the possibility of sexual play. She said I need to listen and trust myself and God and be patient. It's very hard, but my other alternative is to leave. Do I want that?

Sunday, March 1st
● *11:43pm* ●

A small miracle is happening. I realized that a great deal of the fear was my little girl projecting marriage and not accepting my limitations. I've been praying to God. I asked for the courage to trust in God and respect my limitations. Mel and I went to a dinner party last night and then he slept over. We slept until 4:30 in the morning from 11:30 last night. We fooled around and we were then able to sleep until 8:40 when we resumed fooling around. I started flirting with him and I'm glad. I finally told him I was on the pill, so it was one less thing we had to worry about.

While fooling around, I was able to give him a blow job without gagging or feeling gross. I did it a little bit – it was a start. Then he was lying on top of me, and his penis was on top of my vagina and he was rubbing it against me. I was very excited and very aroused, my body was ready for sex, and because I was so ready I got scared and just started to shake. Mel stopped moving and held me very tight until I stopped shaking. Earlier in the morning I had a bad dream and was shaking and he simply rubbed my head until I could go back to sleep. I'm learning to accept my limitations and be honest about my fear.

When I realized how close I was to having sex, I started to shake. It's definitely closer than ever before. His body is losing the power to scare me because of his gentleness, his soft touch, the way he looks at me and holds me when I'm scared. When I started to shake, I stopped caressing him. I literally left him hanging and all I could say was that I was so sorry. He said there's nothing to be sorry about, and he caressed my face and hair and held me until I stopped being afraid. I'm really in love with this man. There are just so many qualities I love about him.

I'm overwhelmed with feelings and it makes it very difficult to concentrate on school. My little girl is definitely having backlash and all she wants to do is cry. I'm scared about the workload of school, overwhelmed with feelings of fear, love, lust, and intimacy. I'm listening to my limitations and still having backlash. I'm having nightmares that I can't remember, and yet I continue telling Mel when I'm scared. Everything seems hard and I don't seem to have the energy. I don't know if I'm exhausted because of my emotions or my sex drive. I'm crying as I write this. What I really want is Mel to just hold me, but the truth is he can't take away my fear of finding myself in that childhood situation. While I'm with him, my adult is present, but in his absence I sometimes let my little girl run the show. God, please give me courage and guidance.

Sunday, March 8th
• *9:40pm* •

So many things have happened. Thursday, when I saw Don, I was telling him how I'm having a hard time concentrating in school, that all I want to do is go to Barbados with Mel. Don asked me if I was in love, and I said yes. That was when I realized that being in love is a distraction. I didn't really know it until Don identified it. I was so glad of that realization and it didn't frighten me. I also told Don about writing my first poems on incest and reading them in class. I'm becoming public with it. The response was so positive. Don pulled out my writing and wanted to return it to me. He said I'd need it for my writing, but he'd like copies of it. I started to cry because another phase of terminating has begun. I shared with him how my writing is becoming a reality, and I'm more present in it and in sharing it with others. I realized that for a long time I wanted to be invisible in my writing as well as my life. I came across a goal list I made in January, 1988. I wanted to achieve the following goals:

• be in a healthy relationship with a man

• have a good paying job

• decide if I wanted to go to graduate school

• come to love my family even though some of them are dysfunctional

Today I've achieved those goals – and so much more. On Friday night while driving to Mel's, I was tearful; I realized I was mourning letting go of Don. I sobbed because the shift had occurred. I'd loved and was in love with Don for a very long time, and now that I'm in love with Mel, I've pushed Don further away. I don't view being in love as a trap but as an addition to my life. When I asked Lyn if she knew I was in love, she started teasing me and said she kind of suspected it. I asked her why I was the last to know? Later on Friday night, Mel and I went out to eat, and I told him my realization about being in love with him and not realizing that I wasn't able to concentrate in school because of that. He looked at me and he said that the light bulb just went off in his head when I said that. We just laughed.

Monday, March 9th
• *7:50pm* •

On Saturday morning in Mel's single bed we had sex for the first time. What a monumental breakthrough! I was so surprised at how much easier it was than I had anticipated. I felt no pain, I felt actual enjoyment and excitement. I felt the difference between sex and incest. Initially I wasn't sure if Mel was in me because I don't remember him penetrating me, but the next thing I'm doing is looking right into his face and telling him all the qualities I admire in him. I realize now that I must have lost focus at the moment of penetration, (I guess being afraid it would hurt), but I was then able to stay in the present by focusing on Mel and not on my uncle. I was amazed at the sexual energy required during sex and how damp our bodies became. I was drenched and had his semen on my legs, belly, vagina; it felt like jelly and it actually felt nice. After we'd made love, he stayed inside me, and just held me while we talked.

Later on Saturday afternoon, Mel left me a phone message which said only that he'd found one of my socks and he'd return it to me when he saw me in school. When I listened to that message late Saturday night, I knew Mel was in shock. When I called him Sunday morning, I asked him if he was OK because his message was strange. He said he'd realized that, but he didn't know what else to say.

He said he was overwhelmed by what had occurred Saturday morning. He said in the future, any decisions he makes must be with me in mind. I asked him if we could take this in small stages. We talked about how when we first started dating, the thought of dating other people wasn't really an issue. He said he was amazed at how well we got along, that we haven't yet had a fight. I told him we don't see each other enough to fight, after all we have just enough time for fun. Mel said both of us being in school and not seeing each other very much made us move slower in the relationship, and that's been good.

Later on Sunday evening, Mel wrote me a poem called *Communication*. It describes how he'd called me to tell me I left a sock in his apartment, although he'd wanted to tell me about our growing love and desire. He read the poem he wrote into my answering machine. He made me laugh, and cry, when I listened. All this work towards intimacy has paid off. I'm totally myself in this relationship, and we can talk about anything.

Communication

I called you last night, I wanted to talk.
I told you, you had forgotten your sock
And I could give it back next time we met.
That isn't exactly what I wanted
To say, but that was all I could think of.

You pierce my inarticulate blather
And together we rummaged through the words
That would name our magic carnality
As we walk our love with its baby steps
To the next adventure with both your socks.

On Friday, Mel asked me another question on incest. He said he'd seen a TV show on prostitutes, and a lot of them were incest survivors. He said seeing that show made him go back and read some more. He asked me if I had flashbacks when we were together. I began to explain that some incest survivors are promiscuous and some are sexually repressed; while I was explaining this, I started to lose my breath. I was able to tell him that I don't have flashbacks when we're together, but I do have them a day or two later, that they're caused by fear. He's asking questions as they come up.

Today was rough. I ate sugar on Saturday at my Mom's and then again today. I started to go into denial and pretended I didn't have sex with Mel. I was convincing myself of that because I didn't remember his entering me. That's when I realized I'd split at that point. All in all, my body is fully alive today and I'm back with the living.

When I told Don, he said he wasn't surprised; it was just sooner than he thought it would happen. Right now I'm totally exhausted. It's probably from the sugar. I'm trying not to worry about having flashbacks.

Thursday, March 19th
- *11:15pm* -

The pink cloud finally burst tonight in Don's office. I'd spoken to Lyn about my fears of Mel's depression, and then about how Mel and I were going to try to read *The Joy of Sex* together. She said I may want to ask Don about all this. She said depression affects all areas, and one of the first places it shows up is in bed.

On Sunday we tried to have sex and just couldn't; part of it was that Mel tried to penetrate me too soon, and it hurt, and another part of me wouldn't open up. I just didn't feel safe. I told Don everything about Mel's depression this week. He asked me how his eating habits were, and I said poor in my opinion. Don said the way Mel eats, lives – just a bed and boxes – and doesn't iron his clothes, all indicate great self-neglect. I told Don I wanted to read *The Joy of Sex* with Mel, and Don just flipped. He said I'm trying to get further in the relationship without looking at the boulder in front of me. My eyes burned from crying. He asked where was I going in this relationship. I said I was waiting to find the extent of Mel's depression, that I was unwilling to live with this condition if it was manic depression. After all, I'd lived with it the first sixteen years of my life. Then I started to cry. I told Don that I couldn't have known all this before.

He said Mel's depression is not a sign of my unhealthiness for picking this guy. He said the relationship has been healthy, and was becoming progressively intimate until now. Don suggested I coast for now in this relationship. He asked why I would want to get more sexually involved with someone like Mel, a person suffering from depression.

I can't afford to do that to my recovery. I've been crying so hard because I finally see the truth. I sobbed all the way home; I'll wait because I'm not willing to be sexually intimate with someone who isn't fully available.

March 20th

I called Lyn and told her everything Don told me and she said she was glad that they were both in agreement (as usual).

I told Lyn that Mel doesn't realize how serious this is. She said no, he has a great deal of denial. I told her how Don started asking me questions about Mel's eating patterns, the way his room is kept, how he wears his clothes, if he's anorexic. I told Don to stop asking me questions like these in that cynical tone of voice; to talk to me in a normal voice. Don said his voice didn't change, I was the one whose perception was changing. He was right; the pink cloud has burst, and I have pink sludge all over me. Don said the denial I have is normal in relationships, it was not reflective of my health. The fact that I was able to have sex with little or no backlash meant the viper was dead.

Don also said there seems to be a great deal of self-neglect on Mel's part. He said everyone goes through depression at different times of their lives, but the fact that for Mel it may be cyclical and with drinking episodes in the past is serious. Lyn said Mel's denial is big. Denial is hard to break through. She said there's nothing I can do but wait right now. I started to cry at work on the telephone with Lyn. I told her I'd put Mel in my God box and turned him over to God, but I didn't realize I might have to let go of the relationship as well. That's what my gut tells me: I'm going to have to let go and leave. I'm so confused.

Tonight Mel, Elena, and I went to the movies. On the way to pick him up I was crying to Elena that I'm scared because there are so many unknowns about his depression, his drinking, and I don't want to live this way. When I went to get Mel I suddenly saw him as old, and I was repulsed. While waiting for him I realized I'd made Mel into a perpetrator. I told Elena this and she said she realized I was doing that. She said I'm already leaving the relationship but I don't know what's wrong yet. I realized my fear has shut down everything. It was strange; with Elena around, Mel was talkative, but when I was driving home we were both quiet. When we got to his house, we kissed and petted in the car; in the middle of it, he said he needed to go to bed because he was tired, and I said sure. But I wondered if what was going on was that he was depressed – it was only 11:30. Granted, he's definitely a morning person, but what about passion and lust?

On Saturday we were at school together, and when I met him at 2:00 that afternoon, we were kissing, and Mel said he wished we could just lock the office and fool around. It was tempting, especially since he's usually not verbal like that. Then we went our separate ways to do homework and meet later on. We had a lovely evening. I cooked dinner and Mel and Jessica read and played together. After dinner, Jessica stacked the dishwasher and Mel washed. We all played games together. For a little while Mel and I just kissed and held each other, and I tickled him. It was so cozy, and relaxing, and desirable.

After that, I don't know if I'll be able to keep my resolution of not having sex with him. My body has finally woken up from a trance; all I want to do is have sex. I want this relationship to work, but part of me knows all the problems that exist and other potential ones.

I talked to Lyn. She told me I'm projecting doom and gloom, that the relationship is over. I told her of my concerns about his drinking and she said his therapist might send him to AA because the only criteria is to stop drinking. She said his family background is too vague. The fact that I'm the oldest and he's the youngest is interesting. She said I can't make a decision right now. It's a date at a time, a situation at a time. She said I probably won't be able to have sex because I can't trust him right now.

Monday, March 23rd
● *8:12pm* ●

I took a mental health day. I just got off the phone with Don. I told him I'm anxious, depressed, and crying. Don said I'm exactly where I'm supposed to be. He said my denial is shattered, that I'm now putting some distance in the relationship. He said there are a lot of good healthy parts to the relationship but a few ugly parts are also beginning to show. He said that I would need to be in limbo for a few weeks in order to determine what to do. I told him that I was planning to meet Mel's parents at the end of April. I would take the relationship one date at a time before I made a decision. Don said I would know in a couple of weeks not months.

Lyn said it sounds like my doom and gloom is running my life and zapping me. She said I can't control Mel or the future. She said I'm being asked to detach and let go. I can't make any decisions because there are none to make yet. She said I need to pray for faith and focus on my recovery.

Saturday, March 28
● *3:35pm* ●

On Thursday night, Mel called to tell me about his session with the therapist. He told Mel that his depressions were not manic depressive, but episodal, directly traceable to the things that were going on in his life at the time. He said that some people have depressive personalities, that Mel was one of them. He also suggested that Mel go to therapy, but it was something Mel would have to take time to think about. He also said Mel needs to find a therapist closer to home. I asked Mel if he mentioned his drinking and he said he believed so. I then told Mel that I thought therapy would be helpful, but I would not badger him. Mel said it was something he had to decide for himself. I realized when Mel told me he wasn't manic depressive how scared I had been about that, and yet I was able to tell Mel that. I told him I knew I couldn't live with either alcoholism or manic depression, but on the other hand I loved him; I'd felt I was between a rock and a hard place and was waiting for some resolution. Mel said he felt really relieved about not being manic depressive, and he would never willingly put me between a rock and a hard place. I told him I was glad because I know my limitations; if he was either an alcoholic or manic depressive I would have to leave the relationship. Mel asked me if that would be very difficult to do. I said I don't know, but under no circumstances would I repeat my childhood. I didn't want to ever live like that again.

After we hung up, I started to become anxious. I thought, 'Oh no, now we have to deal with sex,' and I became scared. Part of me wants sex, and part of me is afraid. The fact that Mel's drinking wasn't discussed a lot makes me anxious. Today, while driving with Tricia, she asked me how I felt about what had happened on Thursday when Mel and I spoke. I told her my concerns about Mel's past drinking; I told her that he'd said he never wanted me to see him drunk because he knows my background. Then I told Tricia that Lyn said that wasn't a good enough reason not to drink, but she also reminded me how I drank in college. I vacillate between wanting to rationalize everything and not listening to my gut, or to analyze everything and see only problems, and run away. I'm very scattered, and it's affecting what I eat. Yesterday I ate sugar for the first time in two weeks. I don't know any answers so I'll wait to talk to Lyn and Don. And yet today I'm with Mel just dealing with the moment, talking about school, and kidding around, and everything is OK. Perhaps I'm just afraid of intimacy and don't know it. I might be afraid of making a mistake and being trapped.

Sunday, March 28th

• *9:45pm* •

Today my lack of peace of mind is a clue that all is not well. When the therapist said Mel wasn't manic depressive I wanted to pretend everything was OK, but the fact that Mel is still depressed doesn't explain anything. I got my answers yesterday. We were in bed fooling around for about three hours and we weren't able to have sex. We undressed each other, which was a first, and I did ask Mel to perform oral sex on me, which he did and we played and laughed, but we couldn't have penetrative sex.

I told Mel I guess on some level I didn't feel safe or trust him yet. Mel looked at me and said 'Yvette, it isn't you. Your body is wide open for me – you trust me – you're ready. It's me.' He said that he doesn't get scared when I'm naked; he doesn't get aroused. I told him that I wondered if he found me attractive, thought I was pretty, because I didn't feel passion from him. He told me that he thought I was beautiful, that he thought I knew it.

He said he didn't think this situation was hopeless, that when I'd told him on Thursday that I couldn't live with manic depression or alcoholism, he was shocked that I'd leave. He said he doesn't want me to leave, that he'll go to any therapy or read any book, but he wants me in his life. I was crying as I said 'Mel, you can't not drink or go to therapy for me. Mel, you have to want it for yourself. Because you're worth it, you're special. Doing it for me wouldn't be enough in the struggle and pain of recovery.' Mel said he is doing it for himself, but what's good for me is good for him at this point.

I said, 'Mel, I'm willing to stay around during the long process if you work at it. But, I can't live the life I lived as a child.' He said he'd call the therapist and talk to him. He wanted me to know the truth and that he was willing to do the work on himself. I told Mel that recovery is possible if we face it and work at it. I told him to look at me – I love, and I like myself. I have a sexuality, a wonderful life, and I think I'm pretty. I told Mel all those gifts were as a result of unburying the incest. I told him by unburying the pain I gained my life back, and found out I wasn't crazy. I said, 'Mel, we're both too young to live with all this pain.'

Friday, April 3rd

• *6:10pm* •

Yesterday, I saw Don and told him everything that happened. He said first of all Mel isn't manic depressive or alcoholic, that I must stop diagnosing and just deal with how I feel in the relationship. I told Don I didn't want to be in his office because he was the first guy I had to tell that Mel wasn't always aroused when I had no clothes on. Don said that was a painful thing to hear. He then asked me if Mel was secure in his sexual identity; could he be bisexual? I said I didn't know, but he definitely wasn't secure in his sexuality either way. Don said I had two choices; I could wait or I could leave. He asked me if the past month had been fun, and I said no. He asked me if after six years of therapy, was this the type of relationship I envisioned myself to be in? That's when I started to cry.

Don said that my recovery process has been a sign of hope and I have the desire to live. He said not many people obtain the level of recovery that I've achieved. He said when I walked in, I had no foundation and all Don gave me were the blueprints. Bit by bit I'd built a beautiful mansion of bronze and gold that shimmered. Then, along came this boy who wants to paint my mansion yellow, covering all the bronze and gold. Am I going to let him? By this point, I was sobbing and Don cursed – which made me laugh. I told Don that I'd surrendered and let God pick the guy, and in had walked Mel. We had become friends, we'd waited and got to know each other before having sex, used birth control. We were both tested for HIV. It still didn't work out. I yelled at God 'I played by all the rules and I still lost.' I couldn't stop crying. I asked Don what I should do with all these feeling of love, 'Mel's such a good guy.' Don said my Dad was also a good guy and loving, and he would have made my life hell if I had been his wife.

Don said I'm on the hill and Mel is in the valley, and I'm going to have to walk down the hill because water seeks its own level. Do I want to walk backwards in my recovery? I told Don that my life depends on my recovery. What about people who have been there for me? How can I leave Mel? Don said the people there for me are my friends and therapist. It's a different relationship with a lover. Don asked me what have I sacrificed to obtain my recovery. I had to drive forty-five minutes each way, went to individual and group therapy even when I had only $7 dollars left every two weeks, and I had to postpone dating, sex, changing jobs, graduate school, and care-free fun.

I realized talking to Don that I didn't want to wait for Mel to deal with his stuff; my life has been on hold in one area or another. I can't afford to wait and let my recovery regress for Mel. I realized last night I have to break with Mel. I'll become angry if I have to wait. I don't want to miss one more minute of my life.

All I've done the last three nights is cry. I'm going to miss the touch of Mel's hair, the sound of his voice, the way he kisses the back of my neck, his brilliant mind, his beautiful eyes, his gentle touch, his wonderful sense of humor, his horrific style in clothes. Doing things together. Our future.

Slivers of silver stacked
                        one
                                by
                                        one
                                                over time rebuilt.

Where once ashes a mansion stands
with stained glass windows that let the
mystery of hope both in and out.

The ashes of my soul   barbecued sacrificial lamb
reborn like a potter with his clay
I mortgaged my life to heal
left with cigarettes bought with laundry money
stripped and
                alone wrapped around a pillow.

Then you my dutch boy asked me to wait
while you glue back the puzzle pieces.
My life has had only one snap shot and
now you're trying to blacken the windows

and paint the glitter yellow
I cannot wait for you
I'll rot in rejection and
despair.

Dutch boy, you walk away angry
questioning my love
and maybe wanting a fling
with the girl who drinks beers and
writes poems about cats in the vatican.

A crystal tear streams down my body

Sunday, April 5th

● *2:30ish* ●

Last night was my last date with Mel; we went to the village, walked around, went to a village fair ate, and then we saw the *Live Brady Bunch Show* with Davi Jones. I was able to put our breaking up on the shelf and just enjoy a special day. I knew that I wanted to enjoy every second. He bought me this great bag, which I told him was perfect for holding my key and condoms.

We then went to his house. I sat down and told him all the sacrifices I'd made to achieve the recovery I have today. And it's only since last September that I've begun to live. My life had been on hold so long. I told Mel that he was asking me to put my life on hold while he got his act together in therapy. I said that could take two or three years and I would die if I had to put my life on hold that long; by this time I was sobbing. I grabbed him and begged him to get help or else he would be a very lonely man, that I wanted him to come back to me in two or three years because he's the man I want to marry. I told him I loved him more than any man I ever loved. I told him I wanted him not be filled with pain and depression, that I wanted him to make love to me, that I wanted joy and peace in his life for him. He said he was willing to go to therapy and do all the work but that still wasn't good enough for me. I said, but it was good enough for him. He asked, does that mean if he could make love would everything be OK? I said no. He said he didn't think so. I said that this is about self-esteem, liking yourself, integrity, positive body image, sexuality, and being in love with yourself. There couldn't be a 'we' because there wasn't a whole 'I' in Mel; there were parts that were missing. I told him I want to share my life with all of him – I want it all. I told him that I loved him so much, but that I love myself more.

Mel didn't talk at all. His eyes filled with tears, and he held me while I sobbed and touched his face. He said he didn't understand why I was doing this, and he hoped I wasn't making a mistake.

I have four more classes and then school is out. I drove home, sobbing and cursing God at the top of my lungs, drove to my Mom's and slept there. She held me and listened. It was nice not having to go to an empty house. Today, I felt like someone cut off both of my arms, that there's no inner peace.

Mel had said he'd call me when he'd made the appointment with the therapist, but he wouldn't call me after that. I could call him if I wanted to. I told him to call me when he was done with therapy, and if we were meant to be together we would be, but if not we'd know.

Wednesday, April 8th
• *10:24pm* •

I'm wiped out. It's three days since we spoke and tonight was our first class together, Mel and I. I went over to him to give him his toothbrush, and we decided to talk while I drove him home. That was when he told me that he'd been sexually abused by an older girl when he was fourteen. He said he doesn't want to go to therapy, but he thanked me for breaking his denial. He then asked me where I had seen our relationship going before this last month. I told him, I saw us becoming more serious and intimate, and we would get married. I said maybe now Mel needs to deal with his stuff, and we need to date other people. I also told him that I didn't want to be just his buddy; after all, growing up I was butchy and guys just wanted to be my friend. If I stayed in the relationship I would become his buddy, and I would feel sexually rejected. I told him, I want to be his lover, and that would mean having sex and being his best friend. If I stayed and continued to feel his rejection, it would affect my self image and I would end up hating him. We decided not to drive home, that we're separated – not divorced. We have hope! I'm also feeling a lot of fear. I guess I'm afraid; now we've admitted that we'd like to marry the other person and exposed ourselves, it won't happen. I guess I'm afraid God will take my deepest desire away. I don't know how I can tell that Mel is the one I want to marry, and yet let go and not talk to him until he's worked everything out. God, I don't know what to do, so I'll give up tonight.

Dear Don

I've just looked at the date and realized that I've been with you in therapy for six years! Its even stranger writing this letter today. I've told you in detail about the two conversations I've had with Mel, and right now I feel like the kid at the party who hasn't been given a grab bag present. And I'm standing here picking my nose.

I came to this big realization. I stopped seeing Mel. And thought I could go back to having a crush on you; but it just doesn't work that way. You're not available. I'm over my crush on you, and Mel is the man I want to marry. So, I let go of my love for you, and I turn round and realize the umbilical cord to you finally snapped. I've gone through everything I can possibly go through with you. I realize that it's time to terminate in a few weeks. What does that mean? Sometime in June?

Sunday, April 12th

• *9:34pm* •

I love talking to Lyn, she gives me so much strength. I told her, at this moment I hate both Mel and Don, and want to push them down the steps. I hate the male gender. I also told her that I've eaten everything I'm allergic to and it's affecting my vision. I'm so angry that I'm abusing myself. I'm taking my anger out on myself, and I did nothing wrong. Lyn said it's an unfortunate situation. Is there really anyone to blame? I said Mel knew he had problems before he met me – why didn't he do anything about them before? Lyn said what about all the people in the meetings who stay in denial? The whole concept is that if you don't talk about it, it will go away. She told me that I may not realize it, but in this relationship I gained more than Mel. I was in a loving relationship where I was able to deal with sex, communication, and intimacy. A culmination of my recovery. And I had the strength to walk away from the relationship. Mel was left having to begin his recovery process whereas I'm ending therapy. Mel lost me and has to face himself. Lyn said everything I gained in this relationship was from my Higher Power. She said, if I think it was given, then I've forgotten where I came from. Lyn said my Higher Power has spared me a great deal of pain by my ending this relationship. I need to allow myself to grieve and be angry, but she reminded me there are no guarantees; we simply learn how to cope better.

I was honest with Lyn and realized that I'm like a binge alcoholic when it comes to food. I realized that this is my third absence from work this past month and a half, and it's a downward spiral. I'm depressed, anxious, and out of control. When my self-esteem suffers, I start eating sugar and run away at a break-neck pace from my feelings, and I crash and need to sleep off the sugar. Lyn said I now have the awareness, and I need to keep a daily conscious awareness of how I'm feeling because 'addiction' includes the notion of 'away from the true self'. I told Lyn I haven't worked this hard to wind up in a recovery program for compulsive overeaters. I recognize that I use food as a way of repressing feelings – at work, with my family, and sometimes even at meetings. Lyn said these are all anxiety-producing places.

God, give me the courage and honesty and willingness to not abuse my body with food. Lyn said that my eating and attendance go hand in hand. Higher Power, I didn't stop smoking to become a compulsive overeater.

Thursday, April 16th

● *10:43pm* ●

I told Don about my talks with Mel, and he said he was surprised at how quickly I broke it off. I was able to tell Don I'd started to back off a month before. I asked Don if there was any chance that Mel and I would get together in a few years after he'd dealt with his own recovery. He said no. He didn't think so. He also said I might not like the guy Mel is after therapy. I started to cry a little. It really hurt to hear that. Don said I'll be mourning for some time, but that it should be better by summer. He said he remembers a time when it didn't matter what season we were in, because I was always in so much pain.

I told him about my realization that I'm a binge eater and it affects me like being a binge drinker. Don became very concerned. He said a few years ago he'd warned me about becoming a compulsive overeater; he'd diagnosed me as that and then it stopped. He said that admitting my destructive eating patterns was the most important thing I've said in months – all my talking about my sexuality and dating is worthless if I'm active in an eating disorder. He said I have an incipent eating disorder. He said I could very well wind up in a recovery program for my eating disorder. He said if I lose one more day of my positive life because of my feelings and what I eat, I'll need to get help. He said I didn't go through six years of therapy, and leave Mel, to miss out on one more day of my life, never mind a year or two.

I told Don I was using conscious awareness, just as I did when I stopped smoking. I told him I had things to think about. I also told him that I would like to see him in two weeks, and then once a month, until September. He said I didn't need him to be there while I mourned. He said when I'm in a long-term intimate relationship I might need to return to therapy, but for now I don't need it. He said that terminating is very stressful, and if I start unhealthy behaviours, we may need to go back to every two weeks instead of once a month. I also told him that right now I hate his gender, that I had an anxiety attack Wednesday night, that after all this fucking work I'd still be a spinster.

Don said it was normal to hate his gender, and also to fear being a spinster.

I've just let go of a significant man in my life. I've bought *The Little Prince*, originally to give to Mel. I've decided to keep it. It's a gift for my little girl.

Saturday, April 18th

● *3:41pm* ●

I'm still anxious from last night. I put in a call to Don and spoke to him a little while ago. I'm afraid by getting help for my eating disorder I'll have to give up my link with Lyn. I'm also afraid because I don't know where this recovery path will take me. I told Don, 'Besides, I hate fat people.' Don asked me why. I said I guess I could become one of them. Don told me I was creating a crisis. All I'm doing is going to a meeting today and listening; I don't have to let go of Lyn; all I have to do is show up. Last Thursday, Don and I had spoken about my eating disorder. Yesterday, Lyn asked me to stop the denial and face my illness. She said, just because my father is dead doesn't mean so is the disease. She said, I need to remember my family's history which includes compulsive eating. She said the disease works on the attitudes of the addiction, that addiction has many faces.

Last night I was talking to Mom and I told her that I missed work, and it was from crashing and eating sugar. She stopped and said that for a smart woman I often act really stupid. She said she realized that I have the most self-destructive behavior with food. That's when I told her I was going to be in a recovery program for compulsive overeaters.

April 19th

● *9:18pm* ●

Tonight I went to my first meeting, and I was very emotional during and after the meeting. Most people at the meeting were thin; yet I identified with the compulsion to overeat, repress one's feelings, either by eating sugar or by overeating.

I had this image: my recovery during the past seven years was like a prairie. So many miracles have occurred, but there is a scrap of metal standing in the field – an eyesore – and it is an anorexia/compulsive overeating disorder.

I spoke to Lyn today, and she said I'm making a crisis out of going to these meetings. She said, I don't need to go to thirty meetings in thirty days. I said, 'How about four meetings a week?' She asked me when was I planning to do homework. I told her I need to get involved. She said she thought two meetings a week were enough. She said I've forgotten all that work I've already put into my recovery. I felt so relieved. So, I will start with two meetings a week.

Two unexpected things happened today. My computer was delivered. I set up the whole thing and it's great! Mel called me to tell me he went to see the therapist today for the first time and they're planning to work together. He seemed hopeful. I was so touched that Mel called me. He was on my mind all day.

God

I took Mel's picture off my desk today, so if he's meant to be in my life, let me know in your time.

I've been running around all week, and I'm running away from my feelings. I miss Mel so, so much. In two days we would have been going out six months. I was crying to Don; I feel like I got the fucking boobie prize again – I lost Mel, and gained an eating disorder. Don said the eating disorder has been there all along waiting to be fully activated.

Wednesday, April 29th

● *11:25pm* ●

I got the chance to talk to Mel after class and showed him my poem. And I started to cry because I miss him so much. He's doing so well. He told me he's happy and OK, working with his therapist on issues of shame. Mel said he realizes that we both have major issues of shame. It was so nice to see him. He's already changing. He told me I looked very good, and he kissed and held me and ran his fingers through my hair. I love the way he smells. He asked me to come back.

I told him I can't because for now he needs to deal with

his own issues; when he gets to the relationship issues, if we're together, we'll work on them. I see the changes beginning. I see him gaining in self-confidence. He told me that he's working on everything so that we can get back together. He asked if I felt ugly when I was around him, and I said I didn't. But I would wind up blaming myself for the effects of his own sexual abuse issues. He said he wasn't the only one who had to work things out. I told him about finding help for my overeating, that once he'd left, my eating went out of control. He told me he'd talked to his parents and told them why he was in therapy. I realized that Mel had known he needed therapy, that even if we don't get back together, he'd be a better person for it.

Monday, May 4
● *10:35pm* ●

I came home and Lyn called and confronted me. She said she thinks I'm closing the door on her because I'm terminating with Don. I told her I felt she didn't have time for me. She said most of this is in my head, she thinks there's a block and that I'm still afraid of her. I told her it was strange, but I felt the same way about my mother. With Don and Lyn, I felt as if my parents had died. Lyn said she thinks I need to work on intimacy with women and sex. All of a sudden, I asked myself – why wasn't I able to make amends with Karen?

Karen was the first woman I ever trusted, and she came out as gay, and that fact separated us because of my fear. I keep viewing my mother and Lyn in a similar confused way. I'm also ashamed of my sexual needs and drives. I told Lyn that some of my old shame came up after breaking up with Mel. Lyn said, 'Isn't it interesting; neither Don nor Mel are in the picture right now, and now you need to deal with sexuality and the fear of intimacy?'

I'm exhausted. I keep on seeing fat people, and I'm obsessed with the fact that I look fat like them. I also experienced my disease in action. I ate a bag of chips for a snack, and tonight, before I started to eat, I was mesmerized by the food. That never happened before. Some of these feelings of obesity, shame and ugliness are due to my conversation with Lyn about intimacy with women, fear of intimacy, not knowing about intimacy without sex, fear of abandonment, sexuality and hiding. Hiding behind the food.

I have a date with Mel next Friday – we're going together to our professor's open house, but then we won't see each other until the fourth of July weekend. I told him we would be able to celebrate leaving his job as he asked me to.

Sunday, May 10th
● 11:06pm ●

The pain and tears have resumed from this morning. Then I realized, I was dreading Mother's Day. Once I acknowledged that feeling, I started having trouble breathing because all the pain was building up. I was enraged with my mother, but I was devastated and hurt too. I realize that I'm still holding onto the fact that my mother sent me to Italy and left me there. I stripped, walked into the shower and sobbed for ten minutes. I realize: I think that if my mother was able to leave me, and she's my mother, what makes me believe Lyn wouldn't leave? Lyn isn't even related to me.

I was able to enjoy Mother's Day, and then come back and do homework and chair a meeting. I accomplished so much because I let that pain about my mother out.

Lyn

I have glass around me. It's very thin and close to me – you can come very very near to me, but I've held onto that small percentage which separates us. I'm afraid to show you my hurt. I don't believe anyone will be there to comfort me so I don't express it, even to myself. 'Lyn, I think I have more trust in you than I do in my mother, but I'm afraid to trust you totally. If I trust you with that complete childlike trust and innocence, you won't stay in my life. So I don't trust you completely; but ninety-five percentage of trust ensures that you're in my life; I yearn to trust my mother and you completely, someday. I don't know if I'm capable of that. I desire that commitment to complete intimacy. It's where I'll find love and spirituality, but I also fear it to the point of suffocation. I think I'm at the point where the need is greater than the fear. I still have an ache in my heart that hasn't been filled. It can only be filled by you and my mother. It is the place of intimacy with women. Acceptance of women, loving women.

Monday, May 11th
• *9:03pm* •

I started getting tearful on the way home tonight, and I realized that I'm very sad. It's an aching sadness about my Mom, myself, and Italy. Lyn said I need to accept that my mother wasn't responsible; she sent me to Italy because she thought I'd be protected. I know my mother wouldn't hurt a hair on my head. Lyn said I need to forgive her, and accept my past. I told her that part of this sadness is also my missed opportunities of intimacy. Lyn helped me realize that while Mel was meeting all my intimacy needs, I let go somewhat of my relationships with women. Lyn said it was unbalanced. The only way I'll be able to have intimacy with men and women is by having the awareness and balancing it. Lyn said for today Mel isn't in my life, but I need my women friends whether he's in my life or not. I told Lyn I really miss the women in my life. She said she's heard me state that only since Mel's been out of the picture.

She said there have been a lot of changes and they affect every area of my life. Terminating with Don makes me feel abandonment in childhood, ending my relationship with Mel and starting to pull back from Lyn. Lyn said I must also stop my behavior around food, and break through the barricades to intimacy. She said I let Mel in a lot and he spent much of his time at my place. I haven't let other people, especially women, do that. I need to start inviting people over – women friends too. It's time I learnt to have intimate friends in my own apartment. Lyn said I need to spend more time with my mother here in my apartment. Lyn reminded me that this sadness will pass. Maybe in future I will begin to realize when I'm not being intimate, when I'm pulling away.

I broke down sobbing on my kitchen floor. I'm mourning the lack of intimacy in my life, I'm afraid that Mel may not be the right person for me, I miss being held by him, miss his closeness, his gentleness, his sparkling eyes when he made me laugh. I miss the feeling of closeness. I'm also going through withdrawal of the food.

Friday, May 15th
● *1:10pm* ●

Lyn asked me if I'd thought any more about intimacy and women. I realize that I desperately want intimacy in my life, but am afraid of letting go of control. If I keep control, I won't be dependent on someone, and I won't have to worry about them leaving. I guess I could trust Don so much because I knew eventually the relationship would end. So I didn't have to worry about abandonment. Also, being that intimate with one man or woman, I would become emotionally dependent, and there wouldn't be a back door, an exit. The feeling of being trapped, suffocated and losing myself are what I control by not being completely trusting and therefore intimate. I guess I fear that if I trust my mother one hundred per cent, she'll die; if I trust Lyn one hundred per cent, she'll move away. Mel may make me responsible for everything; he may change and show his true colors if I trust him completely. I'm afraid of losing myself by being totally intimate.

I also realize that I don't socialize with women on a regular basis. I feel safer being intimate over the telephone or while driving. Whenever I have something hard to say, I say it while driving. I'm stopping that behavior. The other issue that comes up is intimacy and manipulation by women. Men I never trusted, so they weren't able to manipulate me. I wouldn't let them that close, but I thought women were safe, and I'd trust them and do almost anything or accept anything, and I would get screwed.

Sunday, May 17th

• *5:34pm* •

Tonight, when I was talking to Tricia, I began remembering how my mother had said she regretted sending me to Italy, how much she had missed me. She would write to me and send me gifts so I wouldn't forget her, and I would know that she hadn't forgotten me. And she was devastated when I came home and was cold towards her. She said she thought I had stopped loving her.

The truth is, I was in shock and traumatized, and couldn't feel anything. I also believed that when I was sent away I was abandoned. Tonight, I realize that my mother didn't abandon me. She never forgot about me. She just wasn't there to protect me. And then I started to remember when I came back from Italy; how when I was in first grade, she kept insisting I was in the wrong section, and how I was ahead of the class even though I didn't speak English; how in second grade she did my homework with me every night, even after cooking and taking care of Vanessa, how she would go to all school functions and helped me study spelling; and how she helped my Dad put together the bicycle when we moved to Queens.

She gave me her love of books and was very protective of her kids; she was home every day until I reached high school; she never understood me, but loved and accepted me. She kept my incest from my Dad for over a year because I asked her to, even though she could have used my Dad for support. She didn't break her promise. My mother has been there more for me in the last four years than most parents of alcoholic families. She gave me money to buy this co-op. I know she doesn't always understand or agree, but she really does love me. It's time to let her off the hook. It's time to forgive her for not having had x-ray vision and not realizing my uncle was a prick. It's time to forgive her for that decision she made twenty-five years ago — to send me to Italy.

I know my mother would have killed my uncle if he were alive. I need to stop punishing my mother and myself for the past.

We may not have many years left together. I love my mother desperately. Today, I'm in control of my life.

Tuesday, May 19th
• *9:41pm* •

Lyn and I were talking about women and intimacy and she said that I'm mourning. She also said that I'm not trusting of her. She thinks it may be due to my unresolved issues with my relationship with Karen. Lyn said I've made several inferences that I wouldn't be surprised if she were to tell me she's gay. She said I have not been able to trust her or any other woman one hundred per cent because of my experience with Karen telling me she's gay. She said that Karen was the only woman I had trusted completely with my little girl and adult, that it was due to my own background that I felt betrayed when she told me she was gay. Karen had waited so long because she was afraid of being rejected; I had run away because I felt this was yet another relationship that seemed intimate and safe and then changed because of sex.

Lyn asked me what my first thought is when I think of falling in love. I said, sex. She talked about Karen telling me she was gay in May, and in September telling me she was in love with me. Lyn asked if Karen ever made a pass at me, and I said, no. So, Lyn suggested, I'm assuming that she was also sexually attracted to me. She said there are phases of being in love. There's the initial attraction when you're inseparable and ignore all warning signs, and there's a level later which is deeper but still high-pitched. Perhaps the physical intensity lessens and real love begins. Lyn said somewhere in all this there is sex. Being in love is not only about sex. It's that deep feeling of being connected, cared for, safe and accepted. While talking to Lyn, I realized I had those feelings with Karen, except for the sexual feelings. I had those for Mel. When his sexual abuse issue emerged I pushed Mel away like I did Karen.

All I know is that I trusted Karen physically, mentally and emotionally. She was brilliant but humble. She never made me feel stupid. Mel is like that too. She was calm and gentle, and would laugh at me when I was self-engrossed. We didn't play too much, but we were starting to learn how. She knew everything about my issues with my alcoholic family until the incest issue began to emerge. Sometimes, I feel that it was her fault that the incest emerged, but then I think of Don and Lyn and I remember how they had known the previous October.

I guess I'm angry because everything was going great with Karen, I had a best friend, and then the sexual issue came up and blew up everything. First my uncle, then Karen, and then Mel. I'm angry because I still confuse love and intimacy with sex. I still feel helpless in those areas, as if I won't be able to protect myself. I'm angry at myself and at Karen because she had hinted earlier that she is gay. I can see that in hindsight: how she told me she almost had sex with one guy, and then with her roommate, who later went with a guy, but I couldn't read the clues.

I feel like I was tricked again. The joke was on me. I was scared at the time because if I didn't realize she is gay, what else would I find out? I ran away because my incest was coming up, but I lost my best friend – the only woman I had trusted since my mother sent me to Italy. And I haven't been able to trust another women that much again. The pain of letting Karen go is surfacing five years later; if I'm completely honest, I miss her terribly. There's a really big hole in my heart. She was my first intimate relationship in recovery, where honesty and feelings were part of my expressing myself to her. I was totally honest and open, like I was with my uncle, but Karen wasn't. I felt deceived then, even though I realize now that she was protecting herself. I wasn't able to feel generous towards her because I hadn't worked yet on my incest issues. I'm sobbing because the loss is so grave; I'm feeling raw.

I can recognize the feeling because it's similar to how it felt not having Mel in my life, when I didn't think there was any hope. I feel the safety and intimacy in Mel's arms that I felt with Karen. They have both seen me in all my worlds: my work, family, friends, being in pain, sharing my recovery, being myself, child and adult. The difference is that I am sexually attracted to Mel and I flirt with him, and I wasn't sexually attracted to Karen. But I still ran away.

The difference, five years later, is that I'm willing to work with Mel through my fear of intimacy, and I know I'm heterosexual. With Karen, I wasn't yet capable of intimacy because I didn't understand the meaning of love. Lyn and Don have taught me to feel and recognize it, but I held back – until Mel. Now, I have to go back to Karen, Lyn, and my mother, and finally, Mel. A piece of me is buried alive with the ending of my relationship with Karen, and I want it back. I don't want to be homophobic. I want a best friend. I want to give Lyn that small percentage I've been holding back. I want to stop running away from intimacy.

Part of me is not totally cemented in my sexuality. I wonder why I'm so homophobic. I think it's because I still confuse love and sex. The need for both is so great that I sometimes think I'll just accept it from anyone who is loving. There is a curiosity in me about lesbian relationships, but I'm not sure about any feeling in me of desire. There's still fear of sex with Mel, because of my past experiences. With Mel, there's definitely desire, but a great deal of fear too.

Saturday, May 30th
● *12:15pm* ●

So much has happened since Tuesday. Lyn and I have gotten so much closer. The block is crumbling. I also saw Don on Thursday, and I read him my writing about Karen. He said I'm homophobic. He said I'm homophobic as many men are. He said his experience is that women for the most part are not as homophobic, and those who are tend not to be extreme. He said homophobic men have extreme responses and assume that a sexual experience with the same sex means they are gay. He said it is sometimes considered that many males will experiment sexually with the same sex between puberty and early twenties, that some women have lesbian encounters later in their twenties and thirties. He said women may experiment, and accept it as part of their life experience, but many men who have a sexual experience with another male early on may assume they are gay for several years. Of course, other men and women who are attracted to people of the same sex as themselves will recognize that they are gay and be comfortable with that.

When I told Don I left Mel at the same emotional stage as when I left Karen, he said it was when I needed to be both emotionally and sexually intimate. I told him I still confuse love and sex, and that I'm afraid to make amends with Karen. I'm still homophobic, but I care for her. I asked Don if maybe I should see him more to work this out. He said, no. He said, I'm not trusting my recovery. I asked him how can I deal with my homophobia. He said I should talk to Karen about it. I told him that my professor, who is working with me next semester, is a lesbian. He said these are wonderful opportunities to work things through.

I want to. I don't want to be homophobic. It's so judgmental, alienating, narrowminded, and cruel. I'll miss out on some great people. Don said that even if I were to experience women sexually, it would be OK, and it wouldn't mean I'm gay.

After Don, I went to drop off a note in Karen's mailbox asking her to give me a call to get together so I could explain a few things and make amends. As I was getting back into my car, she walked up the driveway. I kissed and hugged her, and she invited me to see her new apartment. We chatted for a while and then she said, 'Yvette, I was never sexually attracted to you.' I told her I had a lot of explaining to do.

On the way home, my little girl was very hyperative, but I was able to tell her that she was safe, that just because Karen is a lesbian, it doesn't mean she's going to attack me. My adult felt relieved. The amends were beginning to be made.

June 2nd
• *7:36am* •

I can't believe I forgot the agony I was in during the first year of dealing with incest. Yesterday was a reminder that the wound is still healing. The achiness, the sweats and shakes, the severe exhaustion, these were all emotional trauma reactions to the incest. I got so angry at myself because I didn't recognize the clues and I was pushing myself to work on all this typing. I'm tearful because I felt weak, and frail, from the backlash.

Sunday, June 7th
● *2:30pm* ●

I've been talking to women about their relationships with women and being homophobic. The more I talk about it, the less scary it gets to own the fact that I want and need women in my life. I learn about myself. They're my buddies. They have my body. They understand my descriptions of an orgasm, eating and sexual issues, and women's struggles. The desire to be pregnant, to be understood by their partners and to have their needs met. I told Lyn that I'm mourning missed opportunities with women and feeling the loss. I realize I need to spend more time with Lyn in person, and I need physical intimacy from her. I'm glad I'm mourning the loss. It means that it's very important that I can start getting the needs met.

Christopher called me tonight. He told me that he and Carol are separated, that he's in therapy because he doesn't know if he's gay or not. He struggled with this issue six years ago, and now it has resurfaced. I knew Christopher was going to tell me that. My gut told me so. Christopher is in a lot of pain. He's dealing with the pain of his separation, his sexual identity and his sexual preference. I told Christopher I love him whether he is gay or straight, that I hope he has the courage to deal with this because he is worth it. He's going to therapy twice a week and he's doing all the work.

Christopher was so honest and open with me. I was so glad he trusted me. I also realized what wasn't in Christopher's marriage: trust, listening and communication. I was able to see how much Mel truly loves me. I saw that Mel didn't fully understand why I needed the time and space, but saying he'd wait for me showed his love for me. Mel, my hope is that I won't hold back my love for you. I adore you, love you and respect you.

Sunday, June 14th
● *3:20pm* ●

I was able to make amends with Karen today and she accepted them. I validated her belief that she had done nothing wrong. The interesting part was that she had no memory of telling me that she was in love with me. In addition, I found out that I was the only person she had told she was a lesbian at that time. By the end of our talk I had to go home because I was having trouble breathing. The incest was coming up. In addition, my car stalled four times today. I guess I am going to be given the strength and perseverance to get through this. I'm going to talk to Lyn tonight, and I'm going to turn over my homophobia, and turn my car over by putting it in my God box.

● *11:00pm* ●

I was talking to Lyn about making amends to Karen, about my homophobia and about realizing that I never show my rage and anger to Lyn. She asked me if I was ever molested by a woman. I started to cry and shake and told her I can't deal with any more abuse. I'm going to lose my mind. I realized that I'm homophobic because a woman incested me. She molested me while my family was in Italy.

Monday, June 15th
● *12:33am* ●

I can't see or find my little girl. What have you done to her? I need to hold her, and clean her, and protect her from all of you. How could you hurt her so? What did she ever do to deserve all this abuse? I can't breathe, I can't stop crying. I can't stop crying. I called Lyn because I couldn't stop crying. I'm afraid to remember.

On Family

Only by looking back
clawing at ghosts
and slashing each monster of
childhood rape
can I begin to discover
a little girl who

silently screamed for
26 years.

She sees memories of
rape, blood, violence, betrayal
abuse, torture, and mutilation
All inflicted on her little body
Her older self had to listen and feel
the pain buried alive
Giving words to the memories
Someone finally believed her.

Six years of memories and the
story is ending
Five perpetrators later and
'La Familia' has
shattered
The illusion of them was too costly to
keep.

My nucleus family and I
six in all
They believed her story
More people witnessed the pain
of the past on today.

A trade in:
One's extended family of 52
for safety, freedom, and life
Trust cannot be returned with
stains of blood and shame.

Leaving the cycle
Three generations of incest behind
I walk away

Monday, July 6th

Today I spent the day with Christopher; I feel the real
Christopher is back for the first time since his marriage to Carol.

He shared so much of himself with me. I was so glad it was my turn to be there for him. He shared his pain of his pending divorce. I told him what I thought about his wife, I called her a cobra. We went to a huge store and played with the toys, we went to the Central Park Zoo and then on the Carousel. I hadn't been there since I was a child. I told Christopher I had to find a specific horse. I knew it when I found it. We rode the carousel with my new sunglasses on – they are purple and weird – and we sang along with the organ playing. We spent the day being kids. We also had lunch at 'Planet Hollywood'. It's wonderful having a friend who has known me for fifteen years, only a little less than half my life.

Friday July 10th

• *3:47pm* •

I told Don about everything that has happened since he went on his vacation and I went on mine; he said I'm a miracle. He said that with this additional incest, he's amazed that I'm still able to let Mel, him, Christopher and Lyn close, especially Mel. He said he would testify in a court and do whatever needs to be done.

I also told Mel everything, and he started to cry. He said he wished he'd been there, that he would have protected me. He held me when the sharing got really hard for me to tell him and he rubbed my back, caressed my hair and just held me against his chest. I told him that I've waited a long time for him, and he's my heart's desire. He said he felt very sad for me, and he was angry at my family for hurting me.

I told him I have to accept my limitations for now, and I can't deal with anything sexual because my eating disorder will blow up in my face. I also asked him not to grab me, to make sure I see him approach me because I may strike out in fear. I told him this isn't forever, that I do want to sleep next to him and make love to him, but not today. He told me he loved me and that we had plenty of time.

Afterword

I would like to say 'And they lived happily ever after', but that would not be the complete truth.

Today, I have an exquisite life. I have more love and intimacy in my life than I ever thought possible. It's more than a year since my last journal entry. My relationship with Mel is strong, healthy, and growing in trust and love every day. We support each other in our recovery. I completed my MA in English in June, 1993. I own my own home, can support myself, and am finally becoming intimate with women. These are the gifts, rewards, and accomplishments of recovery; but recovery is also about painful truths.

I had anticipated that in June 1992 I would terminate therapy with Don. As a result of seeking treatment for my eating disorder, I came to learn that I am not only a compulsive overeater but anorexic as well. That explained why I have been thin all my life while on the treadmill of binging and starving.

After two months of abstinence, I began to have flashbacks of childhood incest, except this time the perpetrator wasn't Uncle Marco. From June 1992 to September 1993, I remembered several more family members who had incested me in the States and in Italy from the time of my infancy to my early teens. The last and most painful memory brought forth my father and mother, who were the primary perpetrators in my life and who allowed me to be abused by various members of the family. Three of the perpetrators were women. I finally received the answer as to why I kept Lyn at arms' length even though I loved and trusted her. Lyn is the first healthy woman I have ever had in my life, but until I remembered the abuse, I viewed her subconsciously as a perpetrator. Today my process of healing is teaching me the beauty of women.

Not only were there several more perpetrators, but my family's sexual practices included satanic ritual abuse. So for me today abuse still shadows sex. Although I'm in great pain once again, today I am no longer a victim. In December 1992, I sought legal action against two members of my extended family, but the statutes of limitations prevented me from pursuing a case. I have been labeled crazy by most of my extended family who do not believe me.

With the exception of a few people, I don't experience their defection as a loss. What I have lost in blood family I have gained in my family of choice. After years of struggling to be intimate with Lyn, I now know what a loving friend she is; she never gave up on this relationship. I can finally see Lyn without the shadows of abuse affecting my perception. We have a spiritual bond which has withstood alcohol abuse, incest, satanic ritual abuse, and all with no prior foundation of trust.

My life is exquisite today, except for the bloody stains of my childhood memories that continue to blot my present life. I expect to be in therapy for an extended period of time. Today through my relationship with Mel I am learning that sex is nurturing and life giving, that intimacy is something I can have and give.

This is not how I envisioned my recovery; but my life has been transformed. I have love, support and a self. Today, I am grateful that I am alive, living, sane, and healing.

October, 1993

Bibliography

Barbach, Lonnie Garfield. *For Yourself: The Fulfillment of Female Sexuality.* New York: Doubleday, 1975.

Bass, Ellen and Davis, Laura. *The Courage to Heal.* New York: Harper & Row, 1988.

Beattie, Melody. *Beyond Co-Dependency: And Getting Better All the Time.* Center City, MN: Hazelden Educational Materials, 1989.

Black, Claudia. *Repeat After Me.* Denver: MAC Printing & Publications, 1985.

Blume, E. Sue. *Secret Survivors: Uncovering Incest and Its After Effects in Women.* New York: John Wiley & Sons, 1990.

Bradshaw, John. *Healing the Shame That Binds You.* Deerfield Beach, FL: Health Communications, 1988.

Buscaglia, Leo. and Short, Steven (eds) *Living, Loving, and Learning.* New York: Fawcett Columbine, 1982.

Comfort, Alex (ed.) *The Joy of Sex: A Gourmet Guide to Love Making.* New York: Pocket Books, 1972.

Hutchinson, Marcia Germaine. *Transforming Body Image: Learning to Love the Body You Have.* Freedom, CA: The Crossing Press, 1985.

Maltz, Wedy and Holman, Beverly. *Incest and Sexuality: A Guide to Understanding and Healing.* New York: Lexington Books, 1987.

Whitfield, Charles, L. *Healing the Child Within: Discovery and Recovery for Adult Children of Dysfunctional Families.* Deerfield Beach, FL: Health Communications, 1987.

Woititz, Janet Geringer. *Healing Your Sexual Self.* Deerfield Beach, FL: Health Communications, 1989.